NATHAN BUSENITZ |

GOD

VS.

GOVERNMENT

HARVEST HOUSE PUBLISHERS
EUGENE, OREGON

God vs. Government
Copyright © 2022 by Nathan Busenitz & James Coates
Published by Harvest House Publishers
Eugene, Oregon 97408
www.harvesthousepublishers.com

ISBN 978-0-7369-8632-8 (pbk)
ISBN 978-0-7369-8633-5 (eBook)

Library of Congress Control Number: 2021947103

Printed in the United States of America

22 23 24 25 26 27 28 29 30 / BP / 10 9 8 7 6 5 4 3 2 1

To the dear members of our respective church families at

Grace Community Church, Los Angeles

and

GraceLife Church, Edmonton

CONTENTS

PART 2: OUR STAND

FOREWORD

John MacArthur

In view of recent events, three basic biblical truths must be emphasized. First, the church is essential. Second, the church must gather regularly and corporately. Third, the church is duty-bound to obey Christ even when doing so violates governmental regulations and restrictions. Given the fundamental nature of these New Testament priorities, it's hard to believe they would prove controversial, especially among evangelicals. But here we are. There has been a great deal of both controversy and compromise, which is why the message of this book is so necessary.

A company of believers is not a "church" if they don't gather. The word for "church" in the original New Testament manuscripts is *ekklesia*. Even before the founding of the New Testament church, that word signified an assembly, a gathering of people. It is comprised of two Greek roots that literally mean "called out," and more specifically, it refers to a body of people called out from their homes (or summoned out of a larger group) in order to muster together. Like the English word *congregation*, the concept of a group coming together is built right into the term.

The church specifically comes together *for worship*, but the vital benefits of the assembly include fellowship, instruction, mutual encouragement, and accountability. Believers are commanded not to forsake the assembly (Hebrews 10:25), and that command comes immediately before the New Testament's most somber warning about apostasy. Fellowship and corporate worship are therefore absolutely essential aspects of spiritual health for individual Christians, and they are also (obviously) vital for the very life of the church.

Believers may be forced by illness, imprisonment, warfare, natural disaster, necessary travel, or some other significant emergency to abstain from the corporate gathering *temporarily*. But there is no justification for the entire church to suspend congregational worship on a prolonged basis. Plagues, pandemics, and persecution have frequently (if not constantly) threatened the people of God since that first Pentecost. Never have faithful churches responded to such obstacles by simply shutting their doors for months at a time and declaring distance-learning technologies a sufficient substitute for corporate worship.

Christians in America and other Western democracies have been blessed and privileged to thrive for more than two centuries under governments that formally affirm and have seldom challenged the right of worshippers to assemble freely. But COVID is a wakeup call and a reminder to believers of how tenuous that liberty is. Pastors in supposedly free countries were literally jailed for weeks because they led worship services during the 2020 lockdowns. The example of James Coates, in that regard, serves as a compelling testimony of pastoral courage and unwavering conviction.

Despite court decisions favorable to churches, a strong current of public opinion favors giving governments more power to force churches to comply with restrictions inhibiting attendance, fellowship, and congregational singing. But the world's opposition to the church and her teaching should not catch believers off guard. "Do not be surprised, brethren, if the world hates you" (1 John 3:13). Jesus said, "Because you are not of the world…the world hates you" (John 15:19). We are citizens of heaven—mere sojourners and aliens here in this world (Philippians 3:20). And even the world sees the church that way when we are faithful to our calling.

That is one of the main reasons why the people of God need to come together regularly for mutual encouragement and instruction. Times of crisis and hardship don't make the church assembly expendable; that's when it is most essential for believers to congregate. "We must obey God rather than men" (Acts 5:29).

Faithful churches must assemble even if they have to go underground to do it. That's how churches in the first three centuries survived and flourished despite intense opposition from Caesar. It's how the church in Eastern Europe overcame communist persecution in the twentieth century. It's how many churches in China and elsewhere meet today.

Scripture gives us several examples of godly people who resisted the ungodly tyranny of rulers who hated biblical truth. Under a despotic Pharaoh, the Hebrew midwives "feared God, and did not do as the king of Egypt had commanded them" (Exodus 1:17). Elijah opposed Ahab and was labeled "troubler of Israel" because of the stance he took (1 Kings 18:17). John the Baptist rebuked Herod to his face and ultimately was killed for it (Mark 6:18-29).

Western evangelicals now need to have that same resolve. We need to prepare ourselves for more pressure from the government and more persecution from the rest of society. When COVID has run its course (if it ever does), other crises are already lined up for government officials to exploit, claiming "emergency powers" to assert more and more regulatory authority over the church.

Now is not the time to forsake our own assembling together. The church must be the church—a pillar and buttress for the truth. We cannot cower in fear. We cannot hide our light under a bushel. We are not called to feed the fears of a world that is perishing. We have been commissioned to "go into all the world and preach the gospel to all creation" (Mark 16:15), and we are soldiers in a spiritual war. "The weapons of our warfare are not of the flesh, but divinely powerful for the destruction of fortresses. We are destroying speculations and every lofty thing raised up against the knowledge of God, and we are taking every thought captive to the obedience of Christ" (2 Corinthians 10:4-5).

It is past time for the church of Jesus Christ to confront the prevailing falsehoods of a depraved society and show hopeless people the way to true hope and abundant life. That, again, is why the message of this book is so necessary. We are the Lord's ambassadors, and we must stand confidently in that role, with joy and not fear, in bold unity—and all the more as we see the day of Christ drawing near (Hebrews 10:25).

—John MacArthur

WHY WE
WROTE THIS BOOK

C hristians and churches have become divisively polarized over the issue of compliance with government authority. Because civil powers have, in ways not seen before, acted aggressively and intrusively in usurping control over the kingdom of Christ, believers have had to face the collision of their duty to government authority and their submission to the lordship of Christ. Our purpose is to explain the clear truth of Scripture on this apparent conflict and, based on that, to show the biblical rationale for why our respective churches took a public stand against governmental intrusion. When civil authorities tried to close us down, both Grace Community Church and GraceLife Edmonton insisted on staying open. The question this book answers is *why*?

The focus of this book is not COVID itself. Studies have demonstrated the pandemic was not nearly as deadly as initially projected.[1] At the same time, as with any illness, we believe churches ought to respond to those who are sick with Christlike compassion and pastoral care (cf. James 5:13-14). That has been our attitude since the onset of the outbreak.

Instead, this book is about government overreach—how civil authorities exploited a public health issue to stir up fear and shut down freedom. Our concern centers on the restrictive measures employed by public officials and the effect those regulations had on local churches that wanted to gather in obedience to Christ (Hebrews 10:25). In a place like North America, including both the United States and Canada, religious freedom has historically been a cornerstone of our society. That liberty is now under attack in unprecedented ways.

The pages that follow recount both our stories and the reasons for our stand. Our thesis is simple: When Christ and compliance collide, we must obey God rather than men (Acts 5:29). As you read this book, our prayer is that you will be encouraged to do just that, standing with courage and conviction for the glory of the Lord.

PART 1

OUR STORY

CHAPTER 1

THE GRACE COMMUNITY STORY

Nathan Busenitz

I f someone had told us, in the fall of 2019, that within six months nearly every church in North America would shut down, we would never have believed them. It would have been difficult to imagine a scenario in which government officials could openly bypass religious freedoms, suspend in-person worship services, and force churches to close their doors. But 2020 was a year filled with unexpected twists and turns. Topping that list was the global pandemic.

PANDEMIC

March–April 2020

When the novel coronavirus first appeared in the headlines, it seemed like a distant threat. But by March 2020, it had taken the world by storm. On March 11, the World Health Organization declared the situation a global pandemic. The next day, California governor Gavin Newsom issued a statewide directive, calling for any gathering of more than 250 people to suspend meeting until the end of the month. At that time, little was known about the new virus. The headlines varied in their assessment of the danger, but many presented the situation in apocalyptic terms. News reports sounded like scenes from a science fiction novel or a Hollywood film. We all had a front-row seat to the unfolding drama.

As the situation escalated, society began to shut down. The same day Governor Newsom issued his directive, professional sports leagues like the National Hockey League, Major League Soccer, and Major League Baseball suspended their seasons, either in whole or in part. The days that followed witnessed a systematic closure of anything deemed nonessential. Activities where people gathered were especially taboo.

Despite the public panic, our pastoral leadership team at Grace Community Church was reluctant to stop meeting. The regular gathering of the saints is commanded in Scripture (Hebrews 10:25). The decision to cancel our weekly assembly, even temporarily, was not something our elders took lightly. The email correspondence with our elder team included this update sent on the morning of Thursday, March 12: "There are no plans to cancel church or other meetings. Early this morning, the CA health department *recommended* no meetings with more than 250 people but that is not mandatory. It is quite possible that we will be ordered to close the church. Unless, and until, that happens we will continue to meet. Obviously, those with health issues or who otherwise do not want to be at risk are free to stay home." The email continued with this pastoral word of encouragement: "The overwhelming fear that has gripped this country is sad. But it is also an opportunity to encourage and strengthen the people of GCC. It is also an opening for the gospel in our community. For those who are afraid, [we] cannot imagine a better place to be than at church with God's people reflecting on the providence and goodness of our Savior, Jesus Christ."

Our desire was to meet, as we did every week. But the situation was developing rapidly, and by the time our elders met that evening, the circumstances had changed. Out of an abundance of caution and in deference to the requests of government officials, we decided temporarily to suspend in-person services. On March 15, Grace Community Church opted for a livestream-only service. Pastor John MacArthur preached about the reality of mortality and the hope that comes only through Christ. His message, which focused on Matthew 6:25-34, was a clarion call not to grow anxious, but instead to trust the Lord. The truth of that passage stood in clear contrast to the anxiety of the culture around us. As our congregation watched from home, we were reminded to rest in the care of our heavenly Father as members of His family who have entrusted their futures to Him.

The following week, on March 19, a statewide shelter-in-place order went into effect, and life as we knew it came to a standstill. The situation in California reflected what was happening across the nation as society screeched to a halt. Almost everything closed, from Disneyland to Yosemite National Park. Schools went online; restaurants emptied their dining rooms; and families huddled in their homes to watch the daily health briefings from Washington, DC. Grocery store shelves thinned out as people stockpiled supplies to prepare for the worst. By the end of March, nations like India had gone into full lockdown, and the Tokyo Olympics had been postponed for a year. Here in the United States, a record-breaking number of Americans filed for unemployment benefits. In less than a month, any semblance of normal life disappeared.

When the shutdown began, our political leaders assured us it would be short-lived. But fifteen days to flatten the curve quickly became thirty days to stop the spread. Days dragged into weeks, and weeks into months. The relatively short break we were told to expect evolved into an indefinite delay. As a result, God's people began to suffer. The Christian life is not designed to be lived in isolation, but in community. Believers are members of the body of Christ (1 Corinthians 12:12-26). No part of the body can survive on its own; it requires fellowship with the other members of the body to function, grow, and thrive. Knowing how essential church is to the spiritual health of the flock, our elders recognized the vital need to act. We could not continue, in good conscience, to suspend the weekly gathering of the church.

Of all the shutdowns and bans on in-person gatherings, the most detrimental targeted churches. Whatever danger the virus posed to the well-being of our citizens, the closure of the church in America posed a greater threat. The ramifications became evident within just a few months as civil unrest erupted with no spiritual influence to counter it.

PROTESTS

May–June 2020

The death of George Floyd in May 2020 touched a nerve at the heart of American history and self-identity. The resulting outcry could be heard from coast to coast. After months of being empty, the streets of our cities became filled with crowds of demonstrators. They marched, knelt, and chanted together to show their united opposition to racial injustice.

At Grace Community, Pastor John met with a group of African-American church members and seminary students to hear from them. He was eager to know what was on their hearts and to gain their perspective. They met in his office for several hours and talked openly about what was happening. During that meeting, he asked how our church could best minister the gospel to the black community. Together, they agreed upon five ways we could help. The following Sunday was Father's Day, June 21. Pastor John opened his sermon by recounting those recommendations for our people.[2]

First, we need to make it clear that racism is a sin. It is a form of hate that is contrary to both the law of God and the gospel of Christ. Second, we ought to show compassion to those who have suffered.

Scripture calls us to weep with those who weep (Romans 12:15). Third, we must be ready to listen. When engaging someone with the gospel, we ought to do so within the context of having heard their heart. Fourth, we should use these days as an opportunity to show the love of Christ. In contrast to the hatred tearing society apart, the church ought to be known for its Christlike care. Finally, the men asked our church to support them in their efforts to raise up the next generation of godly fathers. This fifth point set the stage for the rest of that Father's Day message. The exhortation to our whole congregation to raise up a generation of sons who will honor Christ and "act like men" rang out clearly from the text of 1 Corinthians 16:13.

Protests that started in May continued through the month of June. Many of the demonstrations turned violent and destructive. Americans watched in shock as city centers around the nation descended into chaos. The rioting and looting spanned from Washington, DC, to Washington State, with Seattle even losing control of a six-block portion of the city. On June 8, the Capitol Hill Occupied Protest (CHOP) gained control of Seattle's Capitol Hill neighborhood, including the police department's East Precinct. Later dubbed the Capitol Hill Autonomous Zone (CHAZ), the occupation did not end until police cleared out the protestors in early July.

The anarchy in Seattle was representative of the chaos in other metropolitan areas. In New York, high-end retail stores were vandalized and emptied of merchandise. In Portland, the protests lasted for nearly 200 days in a row, often turning destructive after dark. In Minneapolis, the city council pledged to disband the police department altogether. Here in Los Angeles, as in many other cities, the National Guard was deployed to help keep the peace. Pastor John addressed the chaos and violence in a series of sermons, bringing the Word of God to bear on these disturbing developments. He condemned the vandalism and violence as dishonoring to God.

At a time when law enforcement agencies were under attack, with cries to "defund the police" dominating the headlines, our church made a point to support the countless officers who work hard to serve and protect their communities. As a tangible expression of our gratitude, we invited members of law enforcement to come to the church for a free lunch. The In-N-Out burgers served that afternoon symbolized our appreciation. But that was not the only meal provided that day. Each officer was also given a complimentary copy of *The MacArthur Study Bible*.

From the pulpit, Pastor John emphasized that God has ordained vital structures in society to restrain evil and promote good. Those restraining influences include the conscience, the family, the church, and law enforcement. When the culture cancels the influence of those God-ordained structures, the result is devastating. In a June 14 sermon, he explained, "God has put restraints in the world: the law of God written in the heart in the conscience. This culture has completely destroyed that. The second restraint is the family and the authority of parents and the discipline that parents bring to restrain sin in children; and this culture has destroyed that. And the church has fallen on very hard times with its pragmatism and its desire to entertain sinners and make them feel comfortable, so it no longer comes with any force against sin. And we're not at all surprised that the next restraint and the final one standing is the police; and they're under assault."[3] Our church recognized the pivotal role law enforcement plays in maintaining order and keeping the peace (cf. Romans 13:4). To defund the police, as some were suggesting, reflected yet another step in American society's downward spiral into lawlessness (Romans 1:18-32).

The chaos and destruction of the riots also demonstrated the desperate need for the church's influence as a preserving and restraining element in the culture. The Lord Jesus told His followers:

> You are the salt of the earth; but if the salt has become tasteless, how can it be made salty again? It is no longer good for anything, except to be thrown out and trampled

under foot by men. You are the light of the world. A
city set on a hill cannot be hidden; nor does anyone
light a lamp and put it under a basket, but on the lamp-
stand, and it gives light to all who are in the house. Let
your light shine before men in such a way that they may
see your good works, and glorify your Father who is in
heaven (Matthew 5:13-16).

The church is to be both a preserving element (salt) and a beacon
of hope (light) for the unbelieving world around us. But how could
we fulfill that responsibility if our doors remained closed?

PASTORAL CARE
Summer 2020

The violent unrest that dominated the summer headlines evidenced two important realities. First, it exposed the double standard
of government officials, who forbade religious gatherings but openly
encouraged protesters to march shoulder to shoulder through the
streets. The politics of the pandemic had never been more apparent.
In an election year, public health was being used to stir up strife and
advance a political agenda. Though our elders were not insensitive
to potential health concerns, which is why we continued to offer
livestream options for our Sunday services, we were not willing to
keep the church closed for the sake of politics.

Second, the negative effects of the lockdown underscored the
essential need for the church. The destructive nature of the riots
demonstrated this on a broad scale. But there was also the devastating impact of social isolation on the daily lives of individual people. Cases of severe loneliness, depression, and suicide skyrocketed.
Other social problems also intensified, from harmful addictions to
marital and family strife. Our elders witnessed these ill effects on
the society around us and became concerned for the protection of

our church family. Our people had been deprived of the safety and
vitality that comes from the regular fellowship of the saints. For the
sake of their spiritual care, we felt compelled to open the doors of
the church and allow them to gather.

Throughout the month of June, some of our members started
coming to the church campus on Sundays and sitting in the worship
center during the livestream broadcast. Members of law enforcement also came, not to enforce restrictions but simply to hear the
preaching of God's Word. They were drawn to our church because
of the support and care they received. At that time, Grace Community was not officially open. But our people began to show up anyway, motivated by their love for Christ and for one another. Their
persistent eagerness made it clear to our leadership team that we
needed to reopen officially and publicly.

When we finally resumed in-person services, some wondered
why we had ever suspended them in the first place. To answer that
question, our elders published the following response. It serves as a
fitting conclusion to this part of our story:

"The elders of Grace Church considered and independently con-
sented to the original government order, not because we believed
the state has a right to tell churches when, whether, or how to worship. To be clear, we believe that the original orders were just as
much an illegitimate intrusion of state authority into ecclesiastical
matters as we believe it is now. However, because we could not possibly have known the true severity of the virus, and because we care
about people as our Lord did, we believe guarding public health
against serious contagions is a rightful function of Christians as well
as civil government. Therefore, we voluntarily followed the initial
recommendations of our government. It is, of course, legitimate for
Christians to abstain from the assembly of the saints *temporarily* in
the face of illness or an imminent threat to public health.

"When the devastating lockdown began, it was supposed to
be a short-term stopgap measure, with the goal to 'flatten the

curve'—meaning they wanted to slow the rate of infection to ensure that hospitals weren't overwhelmed. And there were horrific projections of death. In light of those factors, our pastors supported the measures by observing the guidelines that were issued for churches.

"But we did not yield our spiritual authority to the secular government. We said from the very start that our voluntary compliance was subject to change if the restrictions dragged on beyond the stated goal, or politicians unduly intruded into church affairs, or if health officials added restrictions that would attempt to undermine the church's mission. We made every decision with our own burden of responsibility in mind. We simply took the early opportunity to support the concerns of health officials and accommodate the same concerns among our church members, out of a desire to act in an abundance of care and reasonableness (Philippians 4:5).

"But we are now more than twenty weeks into the unrelieved restrictions. It is apparent that those original projections of death were wrong and the virus is nowhere near as dangerous as originally feared.[4] Still, roughly forty percent of the year has passed with our church essentially unable to gather in a normal way. Pastors' ability to shepherd their flocks has been severely curtailed. The unity and influence of the church has been threatened. Opportunities for believers to serve and minister to one another have been missed. And the suffering of Christians who are troubled, fearful, distressed, infirm, or otherwise in urgent need of fellowship and encouragement has been magnified beyond anything that could reasonably be considered just or necessary. Major public events that were planned for 2021 are already being canceled, signaling that officials are preparing to keep restrictions in place into next year and beyond. That forces churches to choose between the clear command of our Lord and the government officials. Therefore, following the authority of our Lord Jesus Christ, we gladly choose to obey Him."[5]

CHAPTER 2

WHAT CAN THE RIGHTEOUS DO?

Nathan Busenitz

I t was my first time preaching a sermon exclusively on Zoom. I routinely used the online platform for teaching in a virtual classroom. But preaching to a screen was a new experience. That Sunday morning, after having my morning coffee, I logged on to the meeting for our Sunday school class. With gallery view engaged, I could see into the living rooms of other church families. They sat on couches and around dining tables, also with coffee in hand, ready to engage in the study of God's Word.

When the time came for the message, I began to preach to my computer screen. It felt strange. This was clearly no replacement for gathering in person. Anyone who regularly participates in public speaking understands the dynamics of engaging with a live audience. There is feedback and energy from the congregation. You can tell when you're connecting, and when they are really listening. None of that comes through over a screen. It's just you and your computer.

In spite of the challenges, I sought to encourage our class that morning with truth from the book of Psalms. A couple months later, I would share this same message with our entire church family during a Sunday evening service. The material also found its way into a blog article that was published and distributed in June 2020.

I've reproduced the content of that message here because it provides a window into what was happening during that season. These were words of encouragement for my own heart, which I was subsequently glad to share with others. The timeless truth of God's Word provided a timely reminder to trust Him despite the unknowns of this life.

THE ANSWER TO UNCERTAINTY
Summer 2020

Unprecedented. I've heard that word more in the past few months than ever before. Given recent events, it seems like a fitting description. These days are filled with unexpected developments and unanticipated challenges on both an international and individual level.

In such seasons of uncertainty, our hearts can become preoccupied with questions like, *Why is this happening? What are we going to do?* And, *When will it end?* As believers, answering those questions from a biblical perspective is vital. The truth of Scripture redirects our attention away from our circumstances and fixes our gaze on the Lord. In so doing, it transforms our worry into worship as we rest our restless hearts in Him.

FOUR COMMON QUESTIONS

God's Word provides the antidote to anxiety. Many passages address the right response to trouble and trials (for example, Matthew 6:25-34; Romans 5:1-5; Philippians 4:6-7; James 1:2-4). In this message, we will consider a group of psalms that articulate the questions we naturally ask in unsettling times. Psalms 10–13 each express the heartfelt concerns of the author in response to difficult circumstances. Together, they identify four common questions people ask in the face of uncertainty and hardship. Let's consider these questions one by one.

Why Is This Happening?

In Psalm 10, dismayed by what is happening around him, the author begins with the age-old question, "Why?" The psalmist exclaims, in verse 1, "Why do You stand afar off, O LORD? Why do You hide Yourself in times of trouble?" The subsequent verses describe the writer's consternation as he sees wickedness increase, seemingly unchecked. In desperation, he wonders, *Why does God not intervene? Why is He letting these things take place?* Such questions flow from a heart confused and distressed by tumultuous circumstances. In uncertain and chaotic times, our minds can easily reverberate with similar thoughts and emotions. We might find ourselves asking the same question as the psalmist: Why is God allowing this to happen?

What Are We Going to Do?

A second common question is found in Psalm 11. This psalm, written by David, expresses the burdens and sorrows of a man fleeing from his enemies (in this case, King Saul). Undoubtedly exhausted and fearing for his life, David verbalized his distress in verse 3 with this question: "If the foundations are destroyed, what can the righteous do?" The consternation David felt is understandable. He was God's choice to be king; he had courageously defended Israel against Goliath; he had honored Saul at every turn. Despite all of that, he found himself a fugitive, forced to flee in order to survive. The question on David's lips is one we might all ask in difficult days. When everything seems to have been flipped on its head, what are God's people supposed to do?

Where Have the Righteous Gone?

Unlike Psalms 10 and 11, Psalm 12 does not contain an explicit question. But the implicit inquiry of the text is obvious. In verse 1, David offers these words of lament: "Help, LORD, for the godly man

ceases to be, for the faithful disappear from among the sons of men."
Like Elijah in 1 Kings 19:14, David felt like he was alone in standing for truth and righteousness. We might express David's concern
with this question: Where have the godly influences in society gone?
For David, it seemed like they had all disappeared, and he felt their
absence acutely. In our own day, as we witness the moral decline
of the culture around us, our hearts resonate with David's cry for
help. We might find ourselves wondering the same thing David did:
Where have the righteous gone?

How Long Will This Last?

Ever since the pandemic began, a question everyone has been
asking is, "How long will this last?" Though David's situation was
clearly different, he asked that same question four times in Psalm 13.
Here is how he expressed it:

> How long, O LORD? Will You forget me forever?
> How long will You hide Your face from me?
> How long shall I take counsel in my soul,
> Having sorrow in my heart all the day?
> How long will my enemy be exalted over me?
> (verses 1-2).

David's repeated question resonates with us because no matter
the trial we are enduring, we are always eager for it to end. Whether
in reaction to an enemy (as in David's case) or in response to health
concerns (as in our day), it is natural to wonder about duration.
And so we may find ourselves asking, How long is this going to last?

ONE COMPELLING ANSWER

As we have seen, Psalms 10–13 articulate four common questions
raised in the face of uncertainty and hardship. It is only natural to
ask these kinds of questions:

- Why is this happening?

- What are we going to do?

- Where have the righteous influences gone?

- How long will this last?

The biblical writers asked those very questions, and we might find ourselves or fellow believers voicing similar lines of inquiry.

But here is a surprising observation: None of these psalms answer the specific questions they pose—at least not directly. Instead, each psalm ends by asking and answering a different and more important question. Rather than engaging questions about *why, what, where,* and *how long,* these chapters turn their attention to the question of *who.* Who is in control? Who is on His throne? Whom should you trust in times of uncertainty? The focus of each psalm shifts from the natural, human point of inquiry to the supernatural, divine sovereignty of God. Therein lies the key to answering our heartfelt questions with heart-changing truth.

Who Is in Control?

In response to each circumstance-driven question, these psalms give a God-centered answer. Psalm 10 began with the question *why?* But it culminates in verse 16 with this declaration of *who* God is: "The LORD is King forever and ever; nations have perished from His land." The psalmist does not need to know *why* things are the way they are. It is enough to know the One who knows all things and sovereignly orchestrates them for His glory and the good of His people.

Psalm 11 asks, "What can the righteous do?" (verse 3) when everything seems like it is falling apart. The next verse responds to that question not with an action plan for what to do, but with a reminder of *who* God is: "The LORD is in His holy temple; the LORD's throne is in heaven." Again, the focus is placed on the person, power, and plan of God.

The implied question of Psalm 12 is, "Where have all the righteous people gone?" Once more, the psalm never gives a direct answer to that question. Instead, David redirects his attention to the truth about *who* God is. Despite his circumstances, David knows he can trust the Lord because God always keeps His word. As verses 6-7 declare, "The words of the LORD are pure words; as silver tried in a furnace on the earth, refined seven times. You, O LORD, will keep them; You will preserve him from this generation forever."

The repeated question of Psalm 13 ("How long...?") is similarly resolved not with a discussion about the duration of difficulty, but by pointing to God's sovereign goodness. The psalm ends with these climactic words: "I have trusted in Your lovingkindness; my heart shall rejoice in Your salvation. I will sing to the LORD, because He has dealt bountifully with me" (verses 5-6). David's sorrow turned to song; his countenance changed dramatically even though his circumstances remained the same. The difference was not in his situation but in his focus. By fixing his eyes on the Lord, remembering *who is in control* and *whom he could trust,* David was able to respond in faith rather than fear.

ASKING THE RIGHT QUESTION

Psalms 10–13 illustrate both the questions we naturally tend to ask in the face of uncertainty and the fundamental question we need to ask if we want to respond rightly. As these psalms demonstrate, we don't need answers to questions about *why* or *how much longer.* As long as we know the answer to *who,* we will never have reason to fear. Armed with the answer to that question, we can face unprecedented days with unwavering courage as our hearts echo the confidence expressed by Paul in Romans 8:31: "What then shall we say to these things? If God is for us, who is against us?"

CHAPTER 3

THE STATEMENT

Nathan Busenitz

T he elders' meeting on the evening of Thursday, July 23, is one I will never forget. "Men, we all need to understand that this is a big deal." With those words, the chairman of our board looked slowly around the room at the forty other elders who had assembled. "I want to go around the room and ask each of you if you are willing to affirm this statement." At that time, we did not know what the implications or consequences might be. Our church would likely be fined. We might possibly be arrested and put in jail. At the very least, we would face criticism for the stand we were about to take. But we understood obedience to Christ is paramount, even if it meant noncompliance with state and local health restrictions.

Several of our elders, including Pastor John, drafted the statement. It was then reviewed by our pastoral staff before going to the full elder board. The statement emphasized that Christ, not the government, is the head of the church. It was a biblical manifesto that made the case that civil government has no authority over the doctrine, worship, or polity of the church. Those matters have been entrusted by the Lord Jesus to His under-shepherds, the pastors and elders of each local congregation (1 Peter 5:4). As we will explain in more detail below, when the government issues mandates that interfere with the church's ability to gather, minister, or worship in a biblical way, it is the church's duty to disobey those injunctions in order to obey Christ.

One by one, each of our elders voiced their affirmation of the statement. It was a sobering moment, like something out of the halls of church history. Some of the men simply said, "I affirm." Others shared additional thoughts and testimony. I referenced Daniel 6 as I explained my decision to affirm. My thoughts went something like this: "When Daniel disobeyed the decree of King Darius, it was not simply because he was commanded to start doing what is wrong; it was also because he was commanded to stop doing what is right. When governing officials tell us we cannot meet as an entire congregation, or we cannot sing in corporate worship, or we cannot fellowship in a biblical way, we must respectfully explain that we cannot comply. To do so would be to stop doing what is right according to what God has commanded in Scripture. And we must obey God rather than man."

That sentiment was shared by the rest of our elder team. We did not know what would happen after that. But we prayerfully entrusted ourselves and our church to the Lord. From that point on, Grace Community Church would publicly open its doors every Sunday. The following day, Friday, July 24, the statement was published on our church's website.[6] If you had visited our homepage that day, you would have seen the following:

Christ, Not Caesar, Is the Head of the Church
A Biblical Case for the Church's Duty to Remain Open
July 24, 2020

Christ is Lord of all. He is the one true head of the church (Ephesians 1:22; 5:23; Colossians 1:18). He is also King of kings—sovereign over every earthly authority (1 Timothy 6:15; Revelation 17:14; 19:16). Grace Community Church has always stood immovably on those biblical principles. As His people, we are subject to His will and commands as revealed in Scripture. Therefore we cannot and will not acquiesce to a government-imposed moratorium on our weekly congregational worship or other regular corporate gatherings. Compliance would be disobedience to our Lord's clear commands.

Some will think such a firm statement is inexorably in conflict with the command to be subject to governing authorities laid out in Romans 13 and 1 Peter 2. Scripture does mandate careful, conscientious obedience to all governing authority, including kings, governors, employers, and their agents (in Peter's words, "not only to those who are good and gentle, but also to those who are unreasonable" [1 Peter 2:18]). Insofar as government authorities do not attempt to assert ecclesiastical authority or issue orders that forbid our obedience to God's law, their authority is to be obeyed whether we agree with their rulings or not. In other words, Romans 13 and 1 Peter 2 still bind the consciences of individual Christians. We are to obey our civil authorities as powers that God Himself has ordained.

However, while civil government is invested with divine authority to rule the state, neither of those texts (nor any other) grants civic rulers jurisdiction over the church. God has established three institutions within human society: the family, the state, and the church. Each institution has a sphere of authority with jurisdictional limits that must be respected. A father's authority is limited to his own family. Church leaders' authority (which is delegated to them by Christ) is limited to church matters. And government is specifically tasked with the oversight and protection of civic peace and well-being within the boundaries of a nation or community. *God has not granted civic rulers authority over the doctrine, practice, or polity of the church.* The biblical framework limits the authority of each institution to its specific jurisdiction. The church does not have the right to meddle in the affairs of individual families and ignore parental authority. Parents do not have authority to manage civil matters while circumventing government officials. And similarly, government officials have no right to interfere in ecclesiastical matters in a way that undermines or disregards the God-given authority of pastors and elders.

When any one of the three institutions exceeds the bounds of its jurisdiction it is the duty of the other institutions to curtail that overreach. Therefore, when any government official issues orders regulating worship (such as bans on singing, caps on attendance, or prohibitions against gatherings and services), he steps outside the legitimate bounds of his God-ordained authority as a civic official and arrogates to himself authority that God expressly grants only to the Lord Jesus Christ as sovereign over His Kingdom, which is the church. His rule is mediated to local churches through those pastors and elders who teach His Word (Matthew 16:18-19; 2 Timothy 3:16–4:2).

Therefore, in response to the recent state order requiring churches in California to limit or suspend all meetings indefinitely, we, the pastors and elders of Grace Community Church, respectfully inform our civic leaders that they have exceeded their legitimate jurisdiction, and faithfulness to Christ prohibits us from observing the restrictions they want to impose on our corporate worship services.

Said another way, it has never been the prerogative of civil government to order, modify, forbid, or mandate worship. When, how, and how often the church worships is not subject to Caesar. Caesar himself is subject to God. Jesus affirmed that principle when He told Pilate, "You would have no authority over Me, unless it had been given you from above" (John 19:11). And because Christ is head of the church, ecclesiastical matters pertain to His Kingdom, not Caesar's. Jesus drew a stark distinction between those two kingdoms when He said, "Render to Caesar the things that are Caesar's, and to God the things that are God's" (Mark 12:17). Our Lord

Himself always rendered to Caesar what was Caesar's, but He never offered to Caesar what belongs solely to God.

As pastors and elders, we cannot hand over to earthly authorities any privilege or power that belongs solely to Christ as head of His church. Pastors and elders are the ones to whom Christ has given the duty and the right to exercise His spiritual authority in the church (1 Peter 5:1-4; Hebrews 13:7, 17)—and Scripture alone defines how and whom they are to serve (1 Corinthians 4:1-4). They have no duty to follow orders from a civil government attempting to regulate the worship or governance of the church. In fact, pastors who cede their Christ-delegated authority in the church to a civil ruler have abdicated their responsibility before their Lord and violated the God-ordained spheres of authority as much as the secular official who illegitimately imposes his authority upon the church. Our church's doctrinal statement has included this paragraph for more than 40 years:

> We teach the autonomy of the local church, free from any external authority or control, with the right of self-government and freedom from the interference of any hierarchy of individuals or organizations (Titus 1:5). We teach that it is scriptural for true churches to cooperate with each other for the presentation and propagation of the faith. Each local church, however, through its elders and their interpretation and application of Scripture, should be the sole judge of the measure and method of its cooperation. The elders should determine all other matters of membership, policy, discipline, benevolence, and government as well (Acts 15:19-31; 20:28; 1 Corinthians 5:4-7, 13; 1 Peter 5:1-4).

In short, as the church, we do not need the state's permission to serve and worship our Lord as He has commanded. The church is Christ's precious bride (2 Corinthians 11:2; Ephesians 5:23-27). She belongs to Him alone. She exists by His will and serves under His authority. He will tolerate no assault on her purity and no infringement of His headship over her. All of that was established when Jesus said, "I will build My church; and the gates of Hades will not overpower it" (Matthew 16:18).

Christ's own authority is "far above all rule and authority and power and dominion, and every name that is named, not only in this age but also in the one to come. And [God the Father has] put all things in subjection under [Christ's] feet, and gave Him as head over all things to the church, which is His body, the fullness of Him who fills all in all" (Ephesians 1:21-23).

Accordingly, the honor that we rightly owe our earthly governors and magistrates (Romans 13:7) does not include compliance when such officials attempt to subvert sound doctrine, corrupt biblical morality, exercise ecclesiastical authority, or supplant Christ as head of the church in any other way.

The biblical order is clear: Christ is Lord over Caesar, not vice versa. Christ, not Caesar, is head of the church. Conversely, the church does not in any sense rule the state. Again, these are distinct kingdoms, and Christ is sovereign over both. Neither church nor state has any higher authority than that of Christ Himself, who declared, "All authority has been given to Me in heaven and on earth" (Matthew 28:18).

Notice that we are not making a constitutional argument, even though the First Amendment of the United States Constitution expressly affirms this principle in its opening words: "Congress shall make no law respecting an establishment of religion, or prohibiting the free exercise thereof." The right we are appealing to was not created by the Constitution. It is one of those unalienable rights granted solely by God, who ordained human government and establishes both the extent and the limitations of the state's authority (Romans 13:1-7). Our argument therefore is purposely not grounded in the First Amendment; it is based on the same biblical principles that the

Amendment itself is founded upon. The exercise of true religion is a divine duty given to men and women created in God's image (Genesis 1:26-27; Acts 4:18-20; 5:29; cf. Matthew 22:16-22). In other words, freedom of worship is a command of God, not a privilege granted by the state.

An additional point needs to be made in this context. Christ is always faithful and true (Revelation 19:11). Human governments are not so trustworthy. Scripture says, "The whole world lies in the power of the evil one" (1 John 5:19). That refers, of course, to Satan. John 12:31 and 16:11 call him "the ruler of this world," meaning he wields power and influence through this world's political systems (cf. Luke 4:6; Ephesians 2:2; 6:12). Jesus said of him, "He is a liar and the father of lies" (John 8:44). History is full of painful reminders that government power is easily and frequently abused for evil purposes. Politicians may manipulate statistics and the media can cover up or camouflage inconvenient truths. So a discerning church cannot passively or automatically comply if the government orders a shutdown of congregational meetings—even if the reason given is a concern for public health and safety.

The church by definition is an *assembly*. That is the literal meaning of the Greek word for "church"—*ekklesia*—the assembly of the called-out ones. A non-assembling assembly is a contradiction in terms. Christians are therefore commanded not to forsake the practice of meeting together (Hebrews 10:25)—and no earthly state has a right to restrict, delimit, or forbid the assembling of believers. We have always supported the underground church in nations where Christian congregational worship is deemed illegal by the state.

When officials restrict church attendance to a certain number, they attempt to impose a restriction that *in principle* makes it impossible for the saints to gather *as the church*. When officials prohibit singing in worship services, they attempt to impose a restriction that *in principle* makes it impossible for the people of God to obey the commands of Ephesians 5:19 and Colossians 3:16. When officials mandate distancing, they attempt to impose a restriction that *in principle* makes it impossible to experience the close communion between believers that is commanded in Romans 16:16, 1 Corinthians 16:20, 2 Corinthians 13:12, and 1 Thessalonians 5:26. In all those spheres, we must submit to our Lord.

Although we in America may be unaccustomed to government intrusion into the church of our Lord Jesus Christ, this is by no means the first time in church history that Christians have had to deal with government overreach or hostile rulers. As a matter of fact, persecution of the church by government authorities has been the norm, not the exception, throughout church history. "Indeed," Scripture says, "all who desire to live godly in Christ Jesus will be persecuted" (2 Timothy 3:12). Historically, the two main persecutors have always been secular government and false religion. Most of Christianity's martyrs have died because they refused to obey such authorities. This is, after all, what Christ promised: "If they persecuted Me, they will also persecute you" (John 15:20). In the last of the beatitudes, He said, "Blessed are you when people insult you and persecute you, and falsely say all kinds of evil against you because of Me. Rejoice and be glad, for your reward in heaven is great; for in the same way they persecuted the prophets who were before you" (Matthew 5:11-12).

As government policy moves further away from biblical principles, and as legal and political pressures against the church intensify, we must recognize that the Lord may be using these pressures as means of purging to reveal the true church. Succumbing to governmental overreach may cause churches to remain closed indefinitely. How can the true church of Jesus Christ distinguish herself in such a hostile climate? There is only one way: bold allegiance to the Lord Jesus Christ.

Even where governments seem sympathetic to the church, Christian leaders have often needed to push back against aggressive state officials. In Calvin's Geneva, for example, church officials at times needed to fend off attempts by the city council to govern aspects of worship, church polity, and church discipline. The Church of England has never fully reformed, precisely because the British Crown and Parliament have always meddled in church affairs. In 1662, the Puritans were ejected from their pulpits because they refused to bow to government mandates regarding use of the Book of Common Prayer, the wearing of vestments, and other ceremonial aspects of state-regulated worship. The British Monarch still claims to be the supreme governor and titular head of the Anglican Church.

But again: *Christ is the one true head of His church*, and we intend to honor that vital truth in all our gatherings. For that preeminent reason, we cannot accept and will not bow to the intrusive restrictions government officials now want to impose on our congregation. We offer this response without rancor, and not out of hearts that are combative or rebellious (1 Timothy 2:1-8; 1 Peter 2:13-17), but with a sobering awareness that we must answer to the Lord Jesus for the stewardship He has given to us as shepherds of His precious flock.

To government officials, we respectfully say with the apostles, "Whether it is right in the sight of God to give heed to you rather than to God, you be the judge" (Acts 4:19). And our unhesitating reply to that question is the same as the apostles': "We must obey God rather than men" (Acts 5:29).

Our prayer is that every faithful congregation will stand with us in obedience to our Lord as Christians have done through the centuries.

THE RESPONSE TO OUR STATEMENT

From the moment it was published, the statement garnered a significant response. Many pastors and churches across the country voiced their affirmation for the stand our elders were taking. They were eager to sign on with us, to show they shared these same convictions. But not everyone was pleased with our approach. Much of the criticism came from expected sources, like mainstream media outlets and secular newspapers. But there was also plenty of friendly fire from other Christian ministries. It came in the form of blogs, social media comments, and private correspondence. Our stand was clearly a polarizing one.

Internally, our elders recognized the need to help our people understand why we were compelled to do this. Many of our members were fully convinced from the beginning. They applauded the decision to reopen the church. But others needed more time to be convinced. We sought to shepherd them with patience and care, as we explained our reasoning from the Scriptures (2 Timothy 2:25). Over the subsequent weeks, Pastor John directly addressed these matters from the pulpit. The rest of our elders also addressed them, both at the fellowship group level and in individual conversations. We emphasized the biblical principles and theological convictions that undergirded our position. During this time, I began to organize those principles into a working document, which was later presented as a seminar at our church. That material, providing the biblical rationale for our position, can be found in chapters 11 and 12 of this book.

CHAPTER 4

LAWSUITS
AND LIBERTY

Nathan Busenitz

I'm so happy to welcome you to the Grace Community Church peaceful protest." With those words on August 9, Pastor John welcomed an auditorium full of congregants. The room erupted in applause. For those not able to find a seat in the worship center, a giant tent in the parking lot provided additional space. The gym and several other classrooms were also needed for the overflow crowd. Livestream options remained available for anyone who preferred to stay home. But most of our members wanted to be together. Their enthusiasm and joy resonated throughout the church campus as God's people gathered to sing praise, hear the preaching of the Word, and participate in corporate worship.

Our church had resumed in-person services a couple weeks earlier, on July 26. Our first Sunday back was two days after the elders published their statement. Pastor John opened his sermon that morning with these words: "This is a very special day in the life of our church family. It is, for us, a return to what we love the most: the fellowship of the saints and the worship of our Lord."[7] He explained that our decision to reopen had received mixed reactions from out-siders. "There have been people all across the country and around the world affirming that we're gathering, thankful that we're gath-ering...And there have been many people who don't understand why we would do this. We understand that. We understand that the world does not understand the importance of the church. The world doesn't understand that it's not just essential, it's the only hope of eternal life for doomed sinners." That truth, that the church is essential, became a rallying cry for our congregation. Our leader-ship team knew how necessary the church is, both as a spiritual ref-uge for the flock and as a gospel witness to the community. Over the subsequent weeks, Pastor John would reiterate this point: "We are simply continuing to do today what we have done for the past 63 years, that Grace Community Church has been open to welcome the Los Angeles community and serve their spiritual needs. We will remain open and teach the gospel of Jesus Christ to all who decide they want to come worship with us."[8]

CEASE AND DESIST
July–August 2020

Our decision to reopen the church quickly caught the atten-tion of officials from the Los Angeles County Department of Pub-lic Health. Three days after our first Sunday back, on July 29, our church received a letter from the county's attorneys. The letter, addressed to Pastor John, began with this paragraph: "The County of Los Angeles (the 'County') has been advised that Grace Com-munity Church held indoor in-person worship services on July 26, 2020. Media coverage of the services included photographs depict-ing hundreds of persons within the Grace Community Church. An online recording of the indoor service is also available on the Church's website. As of July 13, 2020, indoor worship services are prohibited within the County. The County requests that you immediately cease holding indoor worship services or other indoor gatherings, and adhere to the Health Officer Order directives governing activities at houses of worship. If you or Grace Community Church continue to hold indoor services in violation of the law, you are subject to criminal and civil liability."[9] The penalty for violations included a fine of $1,000 per offense and up to 90 days in prison. Each day our congregation met constituted a separate offense.

With county officials pressuring the church to close its doors, our elders turned to legal counsel for help. We found a powerful ally in Jenna Ellis, a senior legal advisor to former President Donald Trump. I first met Jenna when she visited our church on Sunday, August 2. She assured us that we had a strong case not only because of our biblical convictions, but also because of the religious protections guaranteed by the First Amendment. In defending our church, Jenna was joined by a team of attorneys from the Thomas More Society, a not-for-profit law firm specializing in religious liberty cases. They eagerly took our case *pro bono*, and we were profoundly grateful for their help.[10]

On August 12, our legal team filed a lawsuit on behalf of Grace Community Church against state and county officials. The goal of the lawsuit was simple: We were fighting for the right to hold weekly worship services as we had always done. In making our case, our lawyers pointed out that public health restrictions had not been enforced in an equitable way. While governing officials endorsed the right of protestors to assemble for public demonstrations, despite clear health violations, they did not extend those same rights and privileges to churches. This "blatant favoritism" violated the constitutional rights and freedoms granted to churches at both the state and federal levels. Our attorneys also emphasized the negative impact that mandatory isolation was having on society and the church's desire to care for people at such a critical time. As they explained, "With deaths from the 'COVID-19 suicide pandemic' exceeding those from the actual coronavirus pandemic, Grace

Community Church decided that it would no longer sit by and watch its congregants and their children suffer from an absence of religious worship and instruction."[11]

In response, Los Angeles County countersued our church for violating public health orders and requested injunctive releif from the Los Angeles County Superior Court to forbid us from meeting as we had been doing.[12] An initial hearing took place on Friday, August 14. The judge's decision largely favored our church, placing the burden of proof on the county to demonstrate why their attempts to shut down the church were warranted. A full hearing was scheduled for September 4, with the church being allowed to hold indoor and in-person services until that time. The ruling was a great encouragement to our people. Jenna Ellis expressed that sentiment with these words: "This is a huge vindication for Pastor John and the Board of Elders at Grace Community Church, who have simply asked for their right to worship the Lord together in church to be acknowledged and protected…We look forward to continuing to advocate on [their] behalf in asking the Court to protect the fundamental rights of churches."[13]

In making his ruling, the judge asked the church to implement certain health protocols during our worship services while we waited for the full hearing on September 4. Our pastoral leadership team was willing to accommodate that request. But the county refused to accept the judge's decision. The next day, Saturday, August 15, they filed an emergency appeal, and the California Court of Appeal stayed the lower court's ruling.[14] As a result, the ruling from the day before was no longer in effect, and our legal case essentially went back to square one.

The next morning, Sunday, August 16, our church gathered for worship as we normally do. In an interview with CNN from a few days earlier, Pastor John reiterated our church's position clearly: "We open the doors because that's what we are. We're a church."[15] When we continued to meet, the county sought to hold the church in contempt of court. But on August 20, the judge refused to oblige their request. The Court of Appeal had not directly ordered the church to close when it stayed the earlier ruling. It had merely affirmed the county's right to enforce its own health restrictions. Because no other court order was violated, no contempt charge could be brought.[16]

Four days later, on August 24, the county again sought a temporary restraining order against the church.[17] Once more, the judge denied that request, on statutory grounds. Because the Court of Appeal did not grant the county a temporary restraining order when the case came to them (on August 15), and because the situation had not changed since that time, the Superior Court judge was unwilling to grant the county's request.[18] The merits of our case still awaited the full hearing, scheduled for September 4. In the meantime, we continued to trust the Lord and to gather each Sunday for fellowship and worship.

A BOLD DECLARATION
August 23, 2020

In a written declaration to the Los Angeles County Superior Court dated August 23, Pastor John explained the reasons our church was taking its decisive stand.[19] His case centered on the essential nature of the church. He wrote, "The Church's primary function and ministry is providing worship services, training for children, and being a literal sanctuary or refuge for the community. [Since March,] that primary function has been severely burdened and restricted. As a result, after being closed for in-person services for 19 weeks, the Elders of Grace Community Church decided to reopen the church for in-person gatherings."

The declaration continued by recounting the elders' unanimous affirmation of the church's statement, noting that our duty to worship the Lord supersedes the government's authority to prohibit such worship. Executive orders issued by public health officers at both the county and state levels made it impossible for our church to gather corporately for worship. As Pastor John explained, "The worship-bans appear to take the position that we should lock our doors, and force our congregants to gather to worship the Lord in parking lots, in parks, or perhaps beaches—but never in any church. From Grace Community Church's perspective, this is nonsensical, and we view it as a direct ban on engaging in the worship which our faith requires. The size of our congregation means that there is no place for it to meet outdoors; the summer heat makes meeting outdoors unhealthy and even dangerous; our experts have refuted that meeting indoors significantly aids in the spread of the coronavirus; and most principally, Grace Community Church's sanctuary itself is a spiritual refuge for our congregants—a refuge of which the County has no right to deprive them."

He further explained that government bans on worship gatherings "burden my and Grace Community Church's free exercise of religion by criminalizing activity directly required by our faith. As a Church, we have a moral and religious obligation to continue allowing our congregants to gather in our sanctuary to worship the Lord. This church is the core of life for thousands from nursery to seniors. Our church is not an event center. It is a family of lives who love and care for each other in very intensely personal ways—so essential to personal well-being that people rushed back as soon as they could. The utter unnecessary deprivation of all our people by completely shutting down the mutual love and care that sustains our people in all the exigencies, pressures and challenges of life was cruel."

Pastor John's message to the court was consistent with the principles emphasized in the statement from our elders. The gathering of the church is essential for corporate worship, biblical fellowship, and faithful shepherding. Out of a desire to honor the Lord Jesus, we had no choice but to open our doors. For governing authorities to forbid our people from gathering was not only cruel, it was an abuse of power that was both unbiblical and unconstitutional.

THE DRAMA CONTINUES
Fall 2020

In the subsequent weeks, the legal battle between the county and the church continued. On August 28, in what appeared to be an act of retaliation, the county notified the church that it was terminating the church's parking lot lease, effective October 1—a lease that had been in place since 1975. Jenna Ellis responded to the cancellation of the lease with these words: "Los Angeles County is retaliating against Grace Community Church for simply exercising their constitutionally protected right to hold church and challenging an unreasonable, unlawful health order…In America, we have a judicial system to ensure that the executive branch does not abuse its power, and Grace Community Church has every right to be heard without fear of reprisal." She added, "The church has peacefully held this lease for 45 years and the only reason the county is attempting eviction is because John MacArthur stood up to their unconstitutional power grab."[20]

The following week, on September 4, the much-anticipated hearing finally took place. The judge's ruling, published on September 10, was not favorable to our church. He granted the county's request for a preliminary injunction, barring the church from meeting unless our services were fully compliant with county health orders.[21] Our legal team noted the temporary setback but promised to keep fighting for our right to meet in our worship center on Sundays. For his part, Pastor John was undeterred. The following Sunday, September 13, our congregation gathered as usual.

Once more, Los Angeles County sought to hold our church in contempt of court. But again, the judge was unwilling to grant that request, allowing for a trial addressing the church's constitutional concerns to take place first. A September 24 article posted on the Thomas More Society's home page explained what happened: "Los Angeles County has sought to shut down the church and hold MacArthur in contempt, but Thomas More Society attorneys argued that a final determination on the constitutionality of the orders must occur *before* the county could seek contempt against MacArthur for merely holding church." The article continued, "Judge Mitchell L. Beckloff indicated that he agreed there are serious constitutional concerns that have not been fully tried, and he reiterated that his prior ruling on the preliminary injunction was not a decision on the merits regarding the constitutionality of those orders. Because a contempt hearing is a quasi-criminal proceeding, Beckloff agreed that MacArthur and Grace Community Church are entitled to constitutional protections at any such trial."[22]

The ruling was important because it delayed any significant actions by the county against the church until after a trial could be held. We were profoundly grateful for the reprieve and thanked the Lord for His goodness to us. Pastor John's response to the ruling reflected our congregation's resolve: "We are holding church. The Lord Jesus requires us to meet together and we will continue to do that because we are commanded to and because it is our right. I'm very grateful to Judge Beckloff for providing full due process and recognizing the importance of these constitutional protections. The reality is that the county cannot show that their order is even rational, much less necessary. They have also applied their orders arbitrarily and discriminatorily against churches and we enjoy a heightened protection in America to hold church. I'll continue to stand firm and we will continue to fight to protect religious freedom for the church."[23]

On November 13, the next hearing date, the judge set a trial date for January 15, 2021. The intervening two months were pivotal as we rested in the providential care of our heavenly Father. Near the end of November, the US Supreme Court began to issue rulings favorable toward churches in America. Their rulings set important precedents for our case. When January 15 came, the trial date was postponed. It would be delayed several times over the ensuing months. The following month, on February 5, the Supreme Court ruled that California could no longer ban indoor worship services because of the pandemic. The high court also stopped the state's prohibition against congregational singing. These rulings involved lawsuits filed by other churches in California, but they constituted significant victories for our case.

Our trial date was postponed again until June 23. By the time that date arrived, California's coronavirus restrictions had been lifted and there was no longer a need for a trial. A month earlier, in May 2021, Harvest Rock Church of Pasadena won a similar case against the state of California. The result of that ruling was that the state could no longer impose discriminatory restrictions on any church or house of worship. Our leaders at Grace Community Church rejoiced when we heard the news.

At the end of a year-long legal battle, the county's efforts to shut down our church ultimately came to nothing. Despite their threats and intimidation in late 2020 and early 2021, our congregation continued to meet every Sunday for corporate worship without interruption. One detail from that season stands out in my memory. For a number of weeks, health department officials attended our worship services to monitor the situation and cite us for health code violations. They sat in the service, stood for singing and prayer, and clapped when the rest of the congregation applauded. Before leaving, they would issue us a citation. But our people treated them graciously. We were happy to have them join us to hear God's Word preached and His praises sung. In total, thirteen citations were issued between August 30 and November 7, 2020.

The pandemic created unique challenges for churches in America, including governmental pressures never felt before. But Grace Community Church did not merely survive during this season. By God's grace, our church thrived. Attendance grew; giving went up; and opportunities for ministry increased exponentially. More importantly, our church family witnessed the protective power of God, who allowed us to continue meeting when public officials tried to shut us down. For that we give Him all the glory.

Just over one year after the initial lawsuit was filed, on August 31, 2021, the Los Angeles County Board of Supervisors approved a settlement with our church. The county agreed to end its legal actions against the church and to reimburse our legal team for their costs arising from our case. Jenna Ellis issued this statement in response: "The church is essential. Religious liberty and the Constitution won today against the overbroad, arbitrary, indeterminate, and clearly unconstitutional mandates from Gavin Newsom and Los Angeles County. I am so very proud of Pastor MacArthur's steadfast leadership and refusal to abdicate headship of Christ's church to the state. I hope this hard-fought result encourages Californians and all Americans to stand firmly with the protections our Constitution rightly provides, and against tyranny."[24]

Pastor John's words provided a fitting summary of our gratitude to the Lord for His kindness and care to us: "We are very grateful for our Lord's protection and providence throughout this past year. Our commitment to the Word of God and His church has never wavered. We have simply continued to stand firm, as we always have and always will. We put our trust in the Lord Jesus Christ, who is the head of the church. Over the past year, our congregation has seen His hand of blessing in ways like never before, and the Lord's promise has been realized: 'I will build My church, and the gates of Hades will not overcome it.'"

To commemorate the Lord's goodness to our church during this season, a plaque was affixed to the fountain located in the church's plaza. It reads, "To the glory of God for His faithfulness to Grace Community Church in 2020 and 2021." The words of Psalm 91:14-15 are then inscribed:

> Because he has loved Me, therefore I will protect him;
> I will set him securely on high, because he has known
>   My name.
> He will call upon Me, and I will answer him;
> I will be with him in his distress;
> I will rescue him and honor him.

Our prayer is that those words will serve as both a perpetual reminder of God's unwavering faithfulness to His people and an enduring encouragement for our church to stand firm in its commitment to obey God rather than man, no matter the cost.

STANDING IN SOLIDARITY

As we moved into the spring of 2021, our legal battle with Los Angeles County began to move toward resolution. Governmental interference was subsiding. But this was not true for some churches in other parts of the world. One of my good friends serves as a pastor in South Africa. On multiple occasions, due to severe lockdown restrictions, his church was forced to meet in secret. The religious protections granted to South Africans are not the same as what we enjoy in the United States. As a result, his congregation had no choice but to go underground. At one point, he even reached out to pastors in China to learn about their strategies for leading an underground church. It was hard to believe something like that could happen in a Western nation where religious liberties have historically been upheld. But these were strange days.

To hear about a situation like that in South Africa was sobering. But to hear about it in a place like Canada was downright shocking. In the following chapters, you will read the story of what happened to James Coates as he sought to faithfully shepherd GraceLife Church in Edmonton, Alberta. Our elders became aware of his situation and prayerfully supported him from afar.

On February 23, 2021, I posted the following article on The Master's Seminary website.[25] (The Master's Seminary is a pastoral training school that meets on the campus of Grace Community Church.) Titled "We Stand with Pastor James Coates," it reflects our church's appreciation for the courageous stand taken by James and his congregation. It also serves as a fitting segue into the next part of this story:

"The pages of history are filled with examples of faithful believers

who resolutely obeyed God, even if it meant facing severe repercussions from men. When Daniel refused to stop praying, he was
thrown into a den of lions. When the apostles refused to stop proclaiming the name of Jesus, they were arrested and scourged. When
the church father Polycarp refused to renounce Christ, he was burned
at the stake. When the Puritan John Bunyan refused to stop preaching, he was put in jail for twelve years. Many other examples could
be given, but the point is clear. To obey God rather than men is not
always easy. But it has been the heartbeat of believers in every age.

"James Coates is a living illustration of that same kind of resolve.
When government officials interfered with his congregation's ability
to meet and worship, James and his fellow elders determined they
must choose God over government. That courageous stand came at
a cost. James was arrested. When he appeared before the judge, he
was told he would be released if he stopped holding church services
as he had been doing. Like Luther at the Diet of Worms, he respectfully answered that he could not do so. His conscience was bound
to God and Scripture. As a result, James has been imprisoned and
treated like a common criminal.

"It is clear the Provincial Health Authority of Alberta wants to
make an example out of James. We also want to point out his example, because his conduct has truly been exemplary. The faculty, staff,
and students of The Master's Seminary stand in solidarity with
James and his church. He has made us proud. Our desire is to produce men who not only know the content of Scripture, but who live
out biblical convictions. James is that kind of man—a Master's man.
We affirm his courage. But even more so, we applaud the unwavering convictions on which that courage is established. We are trusting
the Lord in all of this, and will continue to pray for our dear brother,
his wife, his sons, his fellow elders, and his congregation. Our prayer
is not only that James will soon be released and restored to his family,
but that as a result of this the message of the gospel will shine forth
to the honor of Christ. Soli Deo gloria!"

CHAPTER 5

THE GRACELIFE
EDMONTON STORY

James Coates

In the fall of 2019, I was in the final year of the Doctor of Ministry program at The Master's Seminary. The program required us, as students, to develop a preaching series delivered in the context of the congregation we serve. My project focused on the theology of preaching, its primacy in the life of the church, and how believers can maximize its sanctifying potential.

In the section on the theology of preaching, I addressed matters like the authority of God, the voice of God, and the presence of God in the preached Word. All of this was intensely relevant for the significance of the corporate gathering. But it was that third component that was most critical—namely, that the preaching of God's Word mediates His presence among His people (1 Corinthians 14:24-25). This conviction is not only both biblical and consistent with the historical Reformation view of preaching, but also elevates the significance of the corporate, in-person gathering.

The net effect of the entire project was that the people in our church not only cultivated a high and proper view of preaching, they also came away with an even greater esteem for the corporate gathering. They understood that the corporate gathering is not an end in itself, but is a critical means for fostering spiritual growth and declaring the glory of God (John 15:8).

THE LOCKDOWN BEGINS
March 2020

When the lockdown began in Canada and restrictions on church gatherings were implemented, my first reaction was one of skepticism. Nonetheless, we initially complied with the restrictions for the following reasons:

First, we were in the same boat as everyone else. We were ignorant with respect to the true severity of the virus. The initial models proposed by leading scientists predicted a pandemic of apocalyptic proportions.[26] Second, we were totally ignorant of the way our legal system works. So when our government threatened the public with fines of $100,000 for the first offense and $500,000 for the second, the consequences for noncompliance were rather compelling. After a second offense, we would have been bankrupt. Third, as we surveyed the landscape of responses coming from the leadership of other respected churches, both in our province and in the US, compliance was the going rate. Under the cumulative weight of those factors, we opted to comply with most of the health orders put in place during the first declared public health emergency.

Our reluctance to do so was evident. On Sunday, March 29, prior to giving my message, I spoke to the congregation for an extended period to address the situation. In that announcement, I noted the tension between Romans 13 and Hebrews 10:25, and said the following: "So we have these two commands in place that [we are] wrestling with and need wisdom to discern when it is that the government is overstepping [its] jurisdiction and [is] therefore infringing on the authority of God; whereby we [must] make a decision whether or not to obey God or man." Our reluctance was so evident that I received an email from a concerned congregant who thought we should be complying with greater eagerness and joy.

Complying with capacity limits required restricting our attendance to 250, then 50, and then 15. In fact, we went from being permitted to have 250 on March 15 to only 15 by March 29. The capacity limit of 15 remained in place until Sunday, May 17 (8 weeks). Because we needed about 7 individuals to make livestreaming possible, we could barely have *a* gathering let alone *the* gathering.

CONGREGATIONAL RESPONSE AND IMPACT
March 2020–June 2020

Our congregation loves to be together, especially on Sundays. We have always been a church that fellowships. Whereas many churches are vacated before the clock strikes noon, our people are together late into the afternoon. If they leave shortly after the service, it is often because they have people coming to their homes. So the notion of "gathering" online did not pass muster for our congregation. Did they make the most of it? Sure. But bringing them back would not be tough.

Our people are also well-informed, both theologically and more broadly. They think critically about culture, politics, medicine, education, and so forth. In many cases, they too had a healthy measure of skepticism toward the government's response to the virus. Some in our congregation believed we should have opened sooner than we did, though they were supportive and submissive in their stance.

Nevertheless, it was incredibly difficult not to be together during those months. In total, we went 14 weeks without gathering corporately. That took a toll on many in our congregation because not only were we not coming together for corporate worship, but the whole world was also coming undone. There was great economic uncertainty, anxiety concerning the future, and an ongoing sense of isolation. In times like that, the body of Christ is vital for encouragement and perseverance. Meanwhile, we were isolating from each other.

SHEPHERDING AN ABSENT FLOCK
March 2020–June 2020

During this time, I was in the early stages of preaching through John 3. That meant preaching John 3:16 to a camera inside of an empty building. Though the feedback from our congregation remained positive, there was one moment that was particularly disheartening for me. My family and I had just arrived home from livestreaming and I was hanging up my suit jacket. I had spent the previous week laboring in the Scriptures. I had just preached my heart out. But I was unable to have any in-person interaction with most of the people entrusted to my care. How were they doing? Were any of them weak? Were any being led into sin? The words of the apostle Paul in relation to such concerns seemed especially relevant (2 Corinthians 11:28-29). I recall expressing out loud to myself, "What in the world are we doing?"

It is impossible to shepherd an absent flock faithfully and effectively. Even preaching itself is designed to be an in-person task. There is engagement and interaction that takes place between the preacher and congregation. The imagery of a shepherd and his flock alone attests to this. How can a shepherd feed an absent flock? How can he protect them? How can he tend to their wounds? We should avoid spiritualizing life in the body of Christ to the point that gathering in person is considered to be of no consequence. Redemption consists of the whole person, both body and soul.

PREPARING TO OPEN
June 2020

Though our church leadership had opted to comply, each of us was active in learning all we could about the pandemic and the way it was being handled. We became convinced the government's response to the virus was an overreaction, and that the virus was not as severe as authorities had originally projected. Alberta Health's own statistics validated this assessment. But we still had not engaged in serious discussion about opening our doors.

Through interaction with another pastor in our province, it occurred to me that I had not yet preached on the matter at hand. I had ministered to our people from the Psalms when the lockdown first began, but I had not yet addressed the issue head-on. So, on the first Sunday in June, I preached a sermon titled "Putting Government in Its Place" from Romans 13. I outlined it around the origin, purpose, and honor of government. I stressed the biblical imperative to be subject to governing authorities. I recognized the implications of surrendering our healthcare system to government control. But I also posed the obvious and pertinent question: Are there any limitations on governmental authority? The biblical answer is clearly yes. When? When obedience to God puts us at odds with government.

If you were to compare that sermon to the second section of this book, you would see a significant degree of continuity—both in identifying occasions when it is appropriate to practice civil disobedience and in articulating the attitude that we should display as followers of Christ. It was that sermon that readied both our leadership and our people to open our doors.

The following Sunday, I preached the other frequently quoted passage in this discussion: Hebrews 10:19-25. I titled it "A Call to Persevere" and framed it around the ground and means of our perseverance. The ground of our perseverance is Christ. The means are threefold: drawing near to God in prayer (Hebrews 10:22), holding fast to the Scriptures (verse 23), and provoking one another to love and good deeds in the corporate assembly (verses 24-25).

In the application tied to the corporate assembly, I emphasized the distinct nature of the corporate gathering, and that at present, we were not gathering corporately (being limited to 50 attendees at that time). I pressed home that a time would come when it would be necessary to gather as the full body of Christ, with or without the blessing of our government and community. I also noted the connection between forsaking the assembly and the risk of apostasy because, in the verses that follow, the author of Hebrews writes one of the severest warnings with respect to falling away. This represents a critical danger. It is something pastors ought to consider seriously as they seek to shepherd their flocks in faithfulness to the Lord.

In response to those two sermons, our leadership and much of our congregation were ready to return to our corporate gathering, in violation of the government's mandates.

FIRST DECLARED PUBLIC
HEALTH EMERGENCY ENDS
June 2020

The first declared public health emergency lapsed in the middle of June and our province's premier (akin to a governor) opted not to renew it. That meant the health orders were no longer legally enforceable. There were guidelines in place for places of worship, but they were just that: guidelines. Though strict capacity limits were removed, the guidelines called for social distancing. So, by default, churches were encouraged to limit their attendees to a number that could ensure everyone remained socially distanced. Nevertheless, we were opening our doors. It was now the choice of each individual to evaluate their own risk tolerance with respect to the virus. Rather than mandate or enforce social distancing, we left that decision up to each congregant.

Our first Sunday open was June 21, 2020. We sent out an announcement on the Friday of that week, and here is what we wrote to our people:

Hello GraceLife family!

After consideration, discussion, and prayer, it is with joy and anticipation that we announce a return to nearly normal services beginning this Sunday June 21st. We are also excited to announce that we will be celebrating the Lord's Supper!

1. As we open our services, it is vitally important that we exercise all diligence in preserving the unity that we have in Christ (Eph. 4:3). For some this is too soon, for others it isn't soon enough. As such, we must extend charity and grace to one another as we navigate the weeks ahead. We must also understand that there are compelling reasons to hold off on returning. Whether it's job related, due to being at high risk, or due to being in regular contact with someone who is, returning to the gathering warrants careful consideration.

2. For those who are returning, it is important that we remain responsible and take reasonable measures to limit the spread of the virus. As such, we're encouraging everyone to hold off on hugs and handshakes for at least the next few weeks. We know this will be difficult, especially given the love and affection we have for each other. But these are prudent steps to take in order to limit any infections. In addition, we must be mindful that some need to exercise greater diligence to socially distance for the reasons noted above and support them in that.

3. Though our prayer is that the Lord would honor this decision to open up our gathering by not allowing any infections, and though infections have the potential to draw negative public attention to GraceLife, we understand that they are nevertheless possible. The Premier of Alberta has acknowledged that in opening up the

province, there will likely be both infections and death. But we also understand this risk to have always been present with influenza and various other viruses. Furthermore, the risk is present every time we leave our home for any reason. Thus, each person must take this risk into consideration in deciding whether or not to return to the gathering. Of course, if you have symptoms, please stay home.

4. In opening up our service, there isn't likely to be sufficient room in the auditorium for social distancing during the structured portion of our gathering (i.e., the service itself). If you would like to return and require sufficient space for social distancing, please register here. The balcony will be designated for this purpose. In addition, the kitchen entrance will be set apart for those accessing the balcony. It provides easy access to the stairs that lead to it. It also facilitates an easy exit as well. Depending on the number of people who register for this option, there may be a weekly rotation similar to what we've been doing for the last few months.

5. As it relates to the current guidelines, it is our understanding at this time that social distancing isn't legally required or enforceable. It is merely recommended. So while we are encouraging everyone to take reasonable steps to limit the spread of the virus, this is coming less from a governmental requirement perspective and more from a place of wisdom and prudence. As we open up our gatherings, we do so anticipating that both COVID-19 and the recommendation to socially distance could be with us for the foreseeable future. This, in part, has contributed to our decision to open up our services. The reasons that could be put forth for not opening may be with us for the remainder of 2020 and not gathering for

that length of time wouldn't be God-honoring in light of His command to assemble and a trust in His sovereign care for His people.

6. Though we're anticipating that some in the body will opt to wait a little longer before returning, we have decided to celebrate the Lord's Supper this Sunday. We are doing so because we recognize that even under normal circumstances, less than the entire body is present for the Lord's Supper. Given that our services are opening up and that we are no longer restricting the number of attendees, we believe celebrating the Lord's Supper is warranted. The temporary cessation of this most wonderful ordinance has been difficult. And so, we intend to remember our Lord in this way this Lord's day. We are taking precautionary measures to ensure that doing so is done as safely as possible.

7. The nursery will remain closed this Sunday June 21st. We will update you of any changes in this regard in the weeks to come.

Regardless of your stance on this decision, please pray that the Lord would honor and bless our gathering. We have largely complied with the government's requests for the last three months. We did this in obedience to Him (Rom. 13:1-7). It is now in obedience to Him that we're opening up our gatherings (Heb. 10:24-25). May God be glorified! May His people be edified! And may love for one another guide and govern all that we do: "Let all that you do be done in love" (1 Cor. 16:14).

CHAPTER 6

CLOSURES AND CONVICTIONS

James Coates

O ur resolve to be open was tested just a few Sundays later. In early July, due to some positive cases and out of an abundance of caution, we decided to close our doors and livestream the service for the next couple Sundays. Here is the announcement we sent on Friday, July 10:

> Dear GraceLife Family,
>
> Given the recent cases of COVID-19 among our congregants, we are going to limit our services to livestream for the next two Sundays. This will allow for any other positive cases to emerge. The tentative plan thereafter is to resume our near-normal services on Sunday, July 26th. Although, we may alter this plan as more information arises.
>
> We are taking this step to slow the spread of the virus. We also do not want to provide any fuel to the narrative that church gatherings are super-spreader events. Thus, by moving to livestream for two Sundays, we believe we

are looking out for the best interests of the congregation, the community, other churches, and the gospel.

Though we cannot and are even loathe to control behavior, we would ask that you socially distance from the body during this period. Doing so should facilitate isolating these initial cases in the congregation and should therefore slow the spread of the virus. It should also allow us to gather on July 26th.

This may be the approach we employ as we seek to slow the spread of the virus for the foreseeable future. As cases emerge in the congregation, we may shift to livestream from time to time.

Lastly, it would greatly assist us if you informed [one of the church leaders] of a positive test result in a timely manner. In fact, it would also assist us to know if you are symptomatic due to contact with anyone who has already tested positive. If you have any other questions or concerns, please direct them to [our leadership].

God is good! We have enjoyed three wonderful Sundays together. It has been such a blessing to gather again. Lord willing, this is merely a short break as we seek to navigate life during the pandemic.

REOPENING OUR DOORS
July 26, 2020

As planned, we purposed to reopen our doors on Sunday, July 26. This decision was essentially settled even though we waited until the preceding Friday to announce it. Coincidentally, the statement titled "Christ, not Caesar, Is the Head of the Church," produced by Grace Community Church, came out the exact same day. So we included it as "An Article of Interest" in our internal messaging.

Reopening our doors this time was more controversial. We received requests for clarification with respect to our rationale for reopening. In the concerns being expressed, some took exception to our inclusion of the statement from Grace Community Church. It gave the impression that our decision to reopen had been influenced by it. Though we found ourselves in total agreement with that statement, this was not the case. When we opened our doors the previous month, we had done so on our own initiative. The same was true this time.

Given the nature of the feedback we received from a number of congregants, we chose to address their concerns and make that response available to everyone. We drafted a document that sought to answer all their questions. It read:

> The following seeks to answer many of the questions that have been raised.
>
> 1. Do we believe the church is being persecuted by the Government of Alberta?
>
> > Thankfully, no. Overall, we are thankful for the way the Premier of Alberta has handled the pandemic in comparison to various other governments. The inclusion of the article by Grace Community Church in our last notification dated July 24th, 2020 was simply an article of interest (as cited). Our decision to open this past Sunday was made internally prior to the release of that statement and was in no way influenced by it. Having said that, we do support the stand they have taken and the rationale for it.
>
> 2. Do we believe that persecution is the threshold that must be met to warrant civil disobedience?
>
> > We do not. Pastor James addressed this quite clearly and directly in his sermon on Romans 13. The

threshold for the practice of civil disobedience is when the government is mandating that we disobey God. In such cases, we must obey God rather than men (Acts 5:29).

3. Why, then, did we comply with the government's prior restrictions on gathering?

We complied with these restrictions due primarily to the initial information on the severity of COVID-19. Though we questioned its severity at that time, we recognized our ignorance in the matter. Complying with the restrictions during the health emergency seemed prudent.

However, as more information was made available, it became clear that initial projections on the severity of the virus were significantly overestimated. With this information and the lapse of the health emergency, we believed it was right in the sight of God to reopen for regular corporate worship.

4. Do we believe the virus should be taken seriously and that it should be avoided?

We believe the virus should be taken seriously. We acknowledge that infection can result in death. As such, reasonable measures should be taken to avoid infection (the kind you would take to avoid influenza). Having said that, we do not believe the virus is severe enough to warrant not meeting as we are currently constituted. In our estimation, governmental restrictions to limit the spread of the virus seem excessive. Though death is certainly a possible outcome of the virus, it is a statistically low probability (https://www.alberta.ca/covid-19-alberta-data.aspx).

The current number for deaths in Alberta is 195 (although a distinction needs to be made between dying with COVID-19 and from COVID-19). As we understand it, most of those deaths have taken place in long-term care facilities (~75%). Furthermore, we understand the average age of those who have died to be 83 (the average life expectancy in Alberta is 81.5). These factors need to be considered when assessing the severity of the virus.

5. Do we believe a livestreamed service constitutes the corporate gathering of GraceLife Church?

We do not. The Greek word for "church" (i.e., *ekklesia*) is a word that in its most basic sense means assembly. Therefore, a non-assembly assembly is a contradiction in terms. However, we are immensely thankful for the technology that facilitates livestreaming and see it as a beneficial stopgap in a season when we are not able to gather.

6. Does the corporate gathering require every member to be physically present for it to constitute the gathering?

On any given Sunday, we have members and regular attendees that are absent. As such, the corporate gathering does not require that every individual be in attendance. However, any restriction that limits the number of attendees such that members and regular attendees are being denied permission to attend alters the nature of our gathering as we are currently constituted (i.e., a body of believers who meet in a single service). Therefore, as leaders, we must determine whether or not the present pandemic warrants denying members of the body permission to attend.

Our aim has been to answer this question in light of Christ as head of His church, since we will give an account for this to Him.

7. Are those who refrain from gathering due to the pandemic in disobedience?

No, not necessarily. Every individual and household must make an informed decision about whether they are willing to assume the risk of gathering. The risk is that you may contract the virus, and this could result in the loss of life. Furthermore, there are work-related issues that need to be considered (e.g., required quarantine periods when a person comes in contact with the virus). There are also matters to consider with regard to being at high risk due to age or comorbidities.

However, there are two matters that need to be addressed. The first pertains to the spirit with which a person chooses to refrain from the gathering. Opting not to attend should be done in humility. As elders, not only are we ultimately responsible and accountable for our decision to open or close our doors, we consider ourselves reasonably informed, both theologically and with regard to the virus itself. Therefore, it is incumbent on every member and regular attendee to respect the decision of the elders, even if you disagree.

The second pertains to our answer to the original question. A time could come when refraining from the gathering is disobedience. At this time, we recognize that there is a lot of conflicting information on the pandemic. As such, we are sympathetic to those who see the severity of the virus differently than we do. But as time passes, its degree of severity will likely be made clearer. Thus, a time could come when abstinence is disobedience to Christ. We encourage everyone to ensure they are well informed. This requires exposing yourself to a broad spectrum of information.

8. Why are the elders not mandating social distancing?

In the first place, we could not gather as a local church and socially distance during our services. Our facility is not large enough. If we were to mandate social distancing, we would have to place a limitation on the corporate gathering that would require denying permission for all to attend. Thus, complying with AHS [Alberta Health Services] guidelines would mean that we cannot assemble as we are currently constituted.

In the second place, we believe social distancing is the prerogative of each individual. We are not here to control behavior or infringe on an individual's personal liberty. Mandating and policing that individuals maintain two meters of separation is beyond the scope of our responsibility. Each person must take ownership and responsibility over the degree to which they practice social distancing. Furthermore, each person must respect the decision of others.

As previously noted, we have made it possible to practice social distancing from the moment a person enters the facility to the moment they leave.

9. Why are the elders not mandating masks?

Again, this is every individual's personal prerogative. It is not our place to mandate masks. Having said that, we heartily support anyone who desires to wear one (as noted by our effort to acquire masks and make them available). In addition, we exhort the body to respect each person's decision whether you agree with them or not. Every individual is responsible to take whatever precautions they deem necessary to feel safe in the gathering.

If the government were to mandate masks, we would not enforce that mandate. We are not the enforcement arm of government. At that point, it becomes a matter of individual accountability to government. (Please note that our church facility falls under the jurisdiction of Parkland County. Thus, the recent vote in Edmonton to mandate masks in public places does not apply.)

10. Have you considered other options (e.g., multiple services, meeting outside, etc.)?

We certainly have. In the case of multiple services, there are many features to consider. For one, moving to multiple services would fundamentally change the way we gather as a body. There would functionally be two gatherings and therefore we would not be gathering all together (it should be noted that we have consistently resisted this change even when numbers reasonably warranted it).

For two, multiple services would place greater strain on the body as it relates to service. It would place additional strain on the sound crew. It would also place additional strain on the music ministry.

For three, it would limit the amount of fellowship that takes place on Sundays. The first service would have to vacate the facility almost immediately.

Fellowship following services is one of the hallmarks of our body.

Fourth, it could limit the preacher's ability to more personally shepherd those who attend the first service. To mitigate this, someone might suggest a morning and evening service. But this, too, would place additional strain on those serving and would fundamentally change the way we are currently constituted.

In the case of services outside, not only is the weather often unpredictable and prohibitive; it is unlikely that everyone would attend and, we would likely have to sacrifice livestreaming for those individuals.

But even if we went with an option like any of the ones touched on above, the next question is how long? It is unlikely that COVID-19 is going anywhere anytime soon. So we would need to be prepared to employ a modified gathering for the foreseeable future (i.e., likely months, if not longer). In our estimation, the virus is not severe enough to warrant that.

11. How have we determined which of the items contained in the "Guidance for Places of Worship" and related public health regulations to observe?

Our approach to Alberta Health has been to take their guidance into consideration and determine what we believe is best for the corporate life of the body. In our estimation, a one-size-fits-all approach is ineffective. Furthermore, there are aspects of our worship that we are not willing to compromise (e.g., singing as per Eph. 5:19 and Col. 3:16). We believe the best thing the government can do is equip us with all the information they have and allow us to make decisions that holistically take the best interests of the congregation into view. AHS is almost exclusively concerned with physical health. We understand that health transcends the physical well-being of a person.

12. Are there any consequences that GraceLife could incur as a result of not complying with the guidelines of AHS?

Potentially, although we do not know what these are. As per our most recent research, the order to practice social distancing is "law." Having said that, the Chief Medical Officer has previously indicated that this law will not be enforced. In addition, we believe it is fair to say that all laws are not created equal (e.g., homicide vs. social distancing). In addition, it is not entirely clear whether government legislation on social distancing would stand up in the court of law.

In closing:

We believe gathering together as a local church is of immense importance to the God and Father of our Lord Jesus Christ. We also believe that the corporate gathering is critical for the spiritual well-being of His people. As such, we believe that faithfulness requires that we open our doors on Sundays and gather in a nearly normal fashion. Having said that, we continue to listen to your feedback, the emergence of new information, and remain open to further consideration and re-evaluation.

You are a precious flock of God and we care for each one of you deeply. In light of this season and recently shifting to livestreaming for two Sundays, we feel like the apostle Paul in his concern for the Thessalonians (1 Thess.

3:1-10). We cannot express how challenging it has been to shepherd you in this season. Flocks are meant to be together, and in some cases, this season has separated us from you. Please know that we love you and want nothing more than for each of you to be thriving in the Lord. Whether or not you agree with our stance, please be diligent to preserve the unity of the Spirit in the bond of peace (Eph. 4:3).

In the Sundays that followed, our attendance steadily grew. But though most of our congregation had returned, there were still a few households who disagreed with our position and believed Romans 13 required that we comply with every governmental regulation. These households were instrumental in helping us refine our thinking. They led us to make sure we could defend the biblical veracity of the stance we had taken and helped us develop the courage and conviction needed for the battle yet to come. Each of these households subsequently left GraceLife amicably. But in hindsight, it became evident the Lord was preparing both our leadership and our church to become a key battleground in the fight to affirm the headship of Christ over His church—a fight that garnered worldwide attention.

CHAPTER 7

THE BATTLE BEGINS

James Coates

O n November 16, we received notification of a complaint pertaining to both Sunday and midweek gatherings at our church. This complaint likely came from a neighbor, possibly an employee of AHS, living in the community adjacent our facility. That same week, the government had asked churches to limit their attendance to a third of capacity, though this request was not mandatory. Rather than administrate limited attendance, we notified our congregation of the government's request and left it to each household to decide how they would respond. Though our attendance was slightly down during the next two Sundays, we were still over the recommended one-third limit.

The following week, I received an email announcing a Zoom call of pastors in Alberta who were concerned about rumors of another lockdown. The stated purpose of the call was "to facilitate the creation of a coalition of churches whose intent is to stay open should the province decide to impose a lockdown." Initially, this was invigorating. A coalition of churches who would stand united against government overreach had the potential for a significant impact. Unfortunately, the various churches had different definitions of what it meant to stay "open."

As I recall, the lockdown was announced the day prior to the scheduled Zoom meeting. This was the second declared public health emergency. Churches were ordered to limit their attendance to a third of capacity. When it came time to unify as a coalition, those who spoke up opposed any sort of stand against the government. They were simply grateful the premier had deemed churches essential, allowing them to stay open albeit at a significantly reduced capacity. When the Zoom call ended, there was no coalition. As a church that sought to remain open without limiting the size of our congregation, we were essentially on our own.

There was a silver lining. During that Zoom call, we were introduced to a lawyer, James Kitchen. James is a tenacious, principled, and historically and politically informed constitutional lawyer. He saw what was happening when the pandemic began and was dismayed by the responses of both churches and the broader public. He joined the Zoom call to equip us to understand our legal protections under the Canadian Charter of Rights and Freedoms. Given my sense that our situation was on the cusp of heating up, I knew I needed to speak directly to him. Soon after, I talked with James over the phone. That connection proved to be providential.

THE GROWING CONFLICT WITH AHS
December 2020

What ensued with Alberta Health Services can be characterized as a staredown. It became more intense on Sunday, December 13. We had already received our first Sunday morning visit from AHS at the end of November. That took place during the Sunday school hour. My interaction with the officer from AHS was reasonably amicable and brief, but I was able to make clear our commitment to a higher, divine authority. One of our elders-in-development managed most of the visit, even engaging the officer in a spiritual conversation. The AHS officer professed to be a churchgoer but had not attended church in some time. That health officer would hear the gospel plenty of times in the weeks that followed.

Leading up to December 13, as had become custom, we sent out an email inviting our people to attend and informing them about what to expect. We let them know that AHS had received another complaint about our gatherings and would likely pay us another visit. We also noted that we had been instructed, by our legal counsel, to refuse them entry, and to do so peaceably.

We found out later that our email was leaked to AHS. As a result, the health officer brought two Royal Canadian Mounted Police (RCMP) along as well. When the RCMP arrived, designated individuals from our church approached them at their vehicles and graciously expressed that we would not be permitting them entrance into our facility on the basis of Section 176 of the Criminal Code of Canada. It reads as follows:

> Obstructing or violence to or arrest of officiating clergyman
>
> 176 (1) Every person is guilty of an indictable offence and liable to imprisonment for a term of not more than two years or is guilty of an offence punishable on summary conviction who
>
> > (a) by threats or force, unlawfully obstructs or prevents or endeavours to obstruct or prevent an officiant from celebrating a religious or spiritual service or performing any other function in connection with their calling, or
> >
> > (b) knowing that an officiant is about to perform, is on their way to perform or is returning from the performance of any of the duties or functions mentioned in paragraph (a)

(i) assaults or offers any violence to them, or

(ii) arrests them on a civil process, or under the pretense of executing a civil process.

Disturbing religious worship or certain meetings

(2) Everyone who willfully disturbs or interrupts an assemblage of persons met for religious worship or for a moral, social or benevolent purpose is guilty of an offence punishable on summary conviction.

(3) Everyone who, at or near a meeting referred to in subsection (2), willfully does anything that disturbs the order or solemnity of the meeting is guilty of an offence punishable on summary conviction.

The attempt to deny entry was unsuccessful. We quoted our code, they quoted theirs, and threatened to arrest anyone who stood in their way. As such, they were able to gain entrance to our facility and joined us for the beginning of our service.

My family and I had not yet arrived. When we did, I admit I was rather unnerved. Seeing police vehicles in your parking lot on the way into the gathering is anything but normal. There was no Sunday school that day, so the beginning of the service was imminent. How was I going to handle this? What should I say? Providentially, it dawned on me what to do. In a time when law enforcement had come under fire, particularly south of our border, it seemed fitting to honor them with a standing ovation. So we did. Then I proclaimed the gospel. It was exactly what many of our people needed to overcome the anger and fear that was in their hearts. As was their custom, AHS and the RCMP left once we started singing. They had the evidence they needed.

On Thursday, December 17, we received an order from AHS. It demanded that we comply with the Chief Medical Officer of Health's orders and threatened further legal action if we failed to do so. Though things were heating up, we were resolved to continue meeting. I had just completed the end of John 8 and because we were approaching the Sunday before Christmas, I would have normally preached an incarnational sermon. At this time, however, I believed a special message was necessary. I sensed it was time to preach a sermon addressing the biblical and theological convictions undergirding our stance. I titled it "The Time Has Come," and its content appears in chapter 13 of this book.

As I delivered that message, it was a bit like an explosion going off. I preached it with full conviction. There was a moment when I pounded the pulpit with the strongest spontaneous compulsion of conviction I have ever experienced in preaching. In fact, it was so strong I had to temper it. When I was done, I sensed I would be a marked man. Just moments following the service, one of our greeters approached and informed me that the RCMP had returned and wanted to see me. As I made my way out of the building, I believed I might be arrested. When I reached the RCMP, they sheepishly handed me a ticket for $1,200. It appeared to me that they did not want to be there and that they were embarrassed.

That sermon had quite an impact on our congregation. There was a buzz in the air and the fellowship that afternoon was sweet. Our attendance had dropped off in the two weeks prior. But thereafter, our church came back with even greater conviction than before. In fact, that sermon was the catalyst for some of our new growth.

WHO IS THE HEAD OF THE CHURCH?
December 21, 2020

I must admit that once the sweetness of our fellowship had come to an end and the dust was settling on that day, a degree of dread came over me. This was unchartered territory. What would happen next? Would I be home for Christmas? Should I be expecting a knock at my door? Even Monday, once it was evident my sermon was getting increased attention, I felt somewhat disconcerted. That is, until the six o'clock news that evening.

We were at the supper table and received a text. It was a video recording of what may have been the leading story that day. The recording included an excerpt from the sermon that was incredibly invigorating. The news anchor introduced it by saying, "In his December 20 sermon, Pastor James Coates of GraceLife Church questioned who had the authority to lead their church, and to decide how or if they can gather." Here is the excerpt they used: "So who is the head of the church? Not Caesar. Not Jason Kenney. Not Deena Hinshaw. Not the lead pastor. Not the elders… The Lord Jesus Christ! Amen." (At the time, Kenney was the premier of Alberta, and Hinshaw was the Chief Medical Officer of Health.)

We could not believe it. The media had used the absolute best excerpt possible. It was thrilling to hear the lordship of Christ heralded like that. It put a gust of fresh wind from heaven in our sails. Nothing provides a more compelling and convicting reason to take a principled stand than the honor and glory of Christ.

THE EYE OF THE STORM
December 27–January 4, 2021

Heading into Sunday, December 27, we were already anticipating we might be locked out of our facility. My sermon from the previous week had garnered about 8,000 views, and we had received a fair bit of media attention. During a staredown, you are constantly trying to anticipate what your opponent might do next. That Sunday, the officer from AHS returned along with the RCMP, but the RCMP remained outside the facility. Our service was conducted without interruption.

Correspondence from AHS typically came on Thursday or Friday of any given week. I often wondered why they waited until then. On the one hand, it could have been to increase the intimidation factor heading into Sundays. It seemed their primary aim was to bring us into submission. So, everything they did was done to secure compliance. On the other hand, it may have taken them that long to decide what to do. We often envisioned AHS in the boardroom flabbergasted as they tried to figure out what to do with us. We were kind, gracious, and respectful, but steadfast, immovable, and courageous.

That week, no correspondence came, and that Sunday, no one visited from either AHS or the RCMP. This brought a much-needed sense of relief. I preached from Daniel 3 and we enjoyed a wonderful afternoon of fellowship. For the moment, we felt as if we had been delivered from our own fiery furnace. But little did we know we were merely experiencing the calm that occurs in the eye of a hurricane. Things would soon get worse.

That Monday, feeling a sense of optimism about the future, I went out and bought a new suit. That might seem like a strange thing to do, but I had some Christmas money from family to spend. The whole experience gave me a thrilling taste of freedom, which I had never realized was so sweet because I had never really noticed it before. I had taken freedom for granted. There was such a degree of darkness looming over us during the preceding weeks that freedom had never felt so good.

In my family, receiving Christmas money is typical, and I had planned to use it to purchase a suit. That seemed like a less-than-frivolous way to use the funds because the suit would serve me in my ministry. But until that weekend, I was in the middle of a dilemma. Would I need a suit in prison? The possibility I might go to prison had already been on my mind. So having a sense of optimism about the future and purchasing a suit believing I would be able to wear it turned out to be an immense blessing.

THE COURT OF THE QUEEN'S BENCH
January 8-21, 2021

Freedom, however, was short-lived. On Friday of that week, our church received a demand letter from AHS detailing our noncompliance. We were told that if we failed to comply with the December 17 order, they would "have no choice but to pursue immediate legal action" against us in the Court of the Queen's Bench of Alberta. Even though that meant the battle was on, it also meant we had at least another Sunday or two together. AHS would need the coming Sunday to determine whether we had complied, and a court date would be scheduled thereafter. We were obviously noncompliant, and the result was a court date on Thursday, January 21.

There is a lot of work that goes into a court appearance. I had to draft an affidavit that detailed both our theological convictions and our response to the virus. This was over and above taking care of the normal rigors of ministry. The hours this battle consumed were too many to count.

Though we felt good about the documents we submitted, we did not expect to win. The Court of the Queen's Bench is not known for being constitutionally strong. As expected, we lost. The court ordered us to comply with the December 17 order from AHS. From there, the tentative plan was to appeal. The challenge with an appeal was threefold: One, it would mean complying with the health orders during the duration of the appeal. Two, the appeal could be as many as six to eight weeks away. And three, there was no guarantee that we would win. Conversely, failing to comply would result in being found in contempt of court; a violation that could lead to as many as two years in jail.

INTRODUCING JACOB REAUME

January 22, 2021

Though the tentative plan leading up to our court appearance was to appeal, our church leadership was already expressing hesitation about this. The idea of complying for as many as two months did not sit well. So, when we lost the court hearing, we knew it was time to figure out what to do next. The next evening, we had a long and draining meeting.

During this season, our leadership team was taking things one week at a time. That meant we had to meet weekly. Much of the discussion during those meetings revolved around whether we would keep going. That, of course, changed after my imprisonment. Once that happened, discussion was no longer needed. We had to keep moving forward.

Something happened the day before that particular Friday meeting. James Kitchen introduced me to Pastor Jacob Reaume of Trinity Bible Chapel in Ontario. I like to think of Jacob as my counterpart in that province. He was the strongest voice in Ontario, and received his fair share of oppression from governing authorities. Jacob and I were on the phone just before our meeting. In that discussion, Jacob indicated his church would be opening their doors that Sunday in contempt of court.

Our church's leadership meeting lasted three to four hours. We considered all the angles. I waited on sharing what Trinity Bible Chapel was doing because I wanted to see where our leadership was at. But after much deliberation, when the time was right, I spoke up. "Jacob and Trinity are opening on Sunday in contempt of court." To which our chairman responded, "Well, we can't let them stand alone." It was settled. We would remain open and risk being found in contempt of court, standing in solidarity with Jacob Reaume and Trinity Bible Chapel.

THE WEIGHTIEST SATURDAY EVER
January 23, 2021

The next day, I was on the phone with James Kitchen. I asked, "How likely is prison time?" Until then, I had considered it rather unlikely. Would they really jail a pastor? Without hesitation, he said, "Pretty likely." Selah. Pause and meditate. That was not what I was expecting to hear. So I asked the next obvious question. "How long?" To which James replied, "A couple of months."

I spent the next two hours digesting that. The physiological impact on my body was considerable. I had difficulty just trying to stand on my own two feet. I felt the weight of the world on my shoulders. I had a migraine brewing and felt fear and anxiety. This would be the cost of following Christ. Changing course was not an option. There was no temptation. I was under what I would call divine compulsion. But I had to settle whether I would be willing to be imprisoned for this.

That day, I settled in my heart that I was willing to go to jail for the stand we were taking. The Lord ministered to me in my weakness, and the nearly unbearable pressure of the moment subsided. Having stared down the barrel of the consequences of the worst-case scenario, my convictions would not allow me to yield, and the Lord carried me through it and out the other side. If the stand we were taking was going to result in my imprisonment, so be it.

CALLING THEIR BLUFF
January 24-29, 2021

In God's providence, I was teaching through John 10 about the Good Shepherd. Scripturally, this was the exact place we needed to be for the moment we were in. We gathered, we worshipped, we fellowshipped, and we waited.

I woke up Friday morning the following week with an email from AHS in my inbox. But it was not what we were expecting.

Instead, it was a closure order, which seemed like a bit of a lateral move on their part. They were ordering us to close our facility to the public until we complied with the current health orders. The stare-down continued. We were putting AHS's political will to the test, and they were not yet ready to jail a pastor.

CHAPTER 8

A MINISTER
IN CHAINS

James Coates

One of the tools the government used to try to bring about our compliance was the mainstream media. Their aim was to paint us in the worst possible light, garner public outrage and animosity, and use that to intimidate us into submission. The media was hammering us, the comment threads were filled with hate and vitriol, and our congregants were beginning to experience opposition from co-workers and extended family members. In light of this, we believed the time was right for a public response.

I began working on a public statement. The aim was not to provide a theological defense of our actions. Instead, I sought to counteract the narrative that we were being selfish and cared little for our community. We wanted Albertans to know that we believed we were doing what was in the best interests of our province. We also made sure to include the gospel.

Timing was critical. We knew our statement would up the stakes with AHS. We waited to see if the media would be back that Sunday, February 7. As I recall, about 15 minutes before the service, there

were already four media outlets taking pictures and video from off
our property. That prompted us to post the statement.

The statement was addressed to our "Dear Fellow Albertans." It
began with this paragraph:

> It goes without saying this has been an incredibly diffi-
> cult 11 months. The effects and ramifications of COVID-
> 19 on our precious province are not insignificant. We
> sympathize with everyone who has suffered loss in this
> time, whether it be the loss of a loved one, or loss stem-
> ming from government lockdowns (such as economic
> loss or suffering as a result of being denied necessary
> health care).

The statement continued by addressing the government's
response to the pandemic. We expressed our view that health officials and the media were manipulating scientific data to create fear
and take control. We further noted the traumatic effects that social
isolation was having on society—effects that, in our opinion, were
more severe than the virus itself. We also lamented the shocking loss
of personal liberty as Albertans willingly surrendered their rights
and freedoms in the face of governmental pressure. We explained
that the command to love our neighbor compelled us to continue
meeting; we were standing for the religious liberties of all Albertans,
not merely those of our own congregants. We encouraged our fellow citizens to return to life as normal. We wrote:

> What do we believe people should do? We believe they
> should responsibly return to their lives. Churches should
> open, businesses should open, families and friends
> should come together around meals, and people should
> begin to exercise their civil liberties again. Otherwise,
> we may not get them back. In fact, some say we are on
> the cusp of reaching the point of no return. Protect the

vulnerable, exercise reasonable precautions, but begin to
live your lives again.

The statement continued by acknowledging that all of life comes
with risks, whether from a virus or from countless other potential
dangers. In light of those risks, we called on our readers to embrace
the Lord Jesus in saving faith. The statement concluded with these
words:

> Human life, though precious, is fragile. As such, death
> looms over all of us. That is why we need a message of
> hope. One that addresses our greatest need. That mes-
> sage is found in Jesus Christ. It is found in Him because
> all of us have sinned and have fallen short of God's per-
> fect standard of righteousness (Rom. 3:23). To sin is to
> violate the holiness and righteousness of God. As our
> Creator, He is the one who will judge us according to
> our deeds, and no one will stand on their own merit in
> that judgment. Therefore, we need a substitute—one
> who has both lived the life we could not and died the
> death we deserve.

> Praise be to God, there is! God the Father commis-
> sioned His Son into the world, to take upon Himself
> human flesh (John 1:14), being true God and true man,
> whereby He lived under the Law of God (Gal. 4:4), ful-
> filled it in every respect, was tempted in all things as we
> are, and yet was without sin (Heb 4:15). Then, in obedi-
> ence to the Father, He went to the cross, drank the full
> cup of the Father's wrath for the sin of all who would
> ever believe on His name, died, and rose again! In this
> way, He proved He had conquered both sin and death,
> our two greatest enemies. He has ascended into heaven
> and is now seated at the right hand of the Father (Col.
> 3:1), awaiting the time of His Second Coming.

In the meantime, this message of salvation is to be proclaimed to all people (Matt. 28:18-20). In fact, the
church exists to proclaim this message! That if you
would turn from your sin and believe on the Lord Jesus
Christ, putting full trust in His finished work on the
cross along with His resurrection from the dead, you
will be saved! Not only will all of your sins be forgiven
you, but you will also be credited with a perfect record
of righteousness; the very righteousness of Christ (2 Cor.
5:21). And so, we would urge you to be reconciled to
God through His Son this day, the very one who has
given you life and breath.

Should you do so, you will receive eternal life and will
experience life after death (John 11:25). Death looms
over all of us. But there is a message of concrete hope in
the gospel of the Lord Jesus Christ.

ARRESTED AND SERVED
February 7, 2021

Given the declarations coming from our premier and Chief
Medical Officer of Health, we sensed enforcement was coming that
Sunday. The mainstream media was pressing them to do something.
The form it would take was anyone's guess, but we knew it was com-
ing. I had packed a change of clothes in case I would be arrested and
taken into custody that day.

For the first time, the RCMP requested access to our facility
without AHS. In an extended conflict like this, change is unnerv-
ing. When I found out, I was shaken. Where was AHS? Why did
the RCMP want to come in on their own? What did this mean?

I was able to pull myself together prior to the announcements.
But it was still apparent I was unsettled. I acknowledged the RCMP's
presence and we gave them a standing ovation, as before. They did

not stay long and left as soon as they had evidence we were not in compliance. Then, after the service, our elder chairman, a former RCMP officer himself, informed me that I would be served with an undertaking and that it was up to me when it happened. Rather than delay the inevitable, I asked to be served right then. The police were back at our facility within 15 minutes.

When the RCMP officers arrived, we went straight to my office. My wife, Erin, was present, along with our elder chairman and a couple of our elders-in-development. I was placed under arrest and served with the undertaking. It required that I agree to comply with the Public Health Act. I knew I could not do that. In place of my signature, the words *Refused to Sign* were entered. Though I had refused to sign, there was still a legal obligation to comply. I was released, and the officers indicated they would be back the following week. That meant they knew we would be too. The interaction was amicable and respectful.

At times, the relentless pressure of the situation produced moments of weariness. But by this point, I had reached a state of endurance where I felt I could go on forever. It was akin to the point athletes reach when they get a second wind. It was a level of spiritual endurance I had never experienced before. The athletic imagery the apostle Paul included in the New Testament became intensely experiential for me. I felt like a spiritual athlete in the race of my life, and I needed to go the distance. Sustained by God's grace, and surrounded by a godly team of elders, we pushed forward, fully entrusting the future to the Lord.

BRINGING GOD'S WORD TO BEAR ON GOVERNMENT
Sunday, February 14, 2021

The next week, I knew I needed to speak to the moment. But before I could turn my undivided attention to preparing that message, I had a funeral to do. We had just lost a life to the pandemic. But we did not lose him to COVID-19. Instead, we lost him to the effects of the lockdown measures. He had been diagnosed with cancer and his second round of treatments had been delayed. From a human perspective, his death was accelerated because of that delay. And he died in isolation from the body of believers he so dearly loved.

It is amazing how strange life had become by this point. I had just been arrested and released for holding a worship service. I was now caring for a family who had lost their believing dad, relative, and friend. I was conducting a forbidden worship service in one moment and caring for people at a gravesite in the next. Did the government really want to treat me like a criminal?

I did a CrossPolitic interview on a podcast called "Waterbreak with The Waterboy" on Thursday afternoon of that week.[27] Normally by this point in the week my preparation for Sunday would have been well underway. But I was still trying to decide what to preach. I leaned toward addressing the issue of government, but from a different angle than in my sermon from the previous summer.

On the day of my first arrest, during Sunday evening fellowship, one of our Bible study shepherds posed some questions that went something like this: "What is the best way for us to call government to its God-given duty? Should we write a letter? Should we phone them? Should we write an open letter on a blog?" His inquiry got my mind going, and I had been pondering the possible answers all week. When Friday arrived, I devoted the day to organizing my thoughts. By the end of the day, the direction had become clear. My time Saturday was spent writing the sermon.

In God's providence, the sermon proved to be very timely. The title was "Directing Government to Its Duty" (you will find this message in chapter 14 of this book). Both this message, and the earlier one titled "The Time Has Come," were pivotal in my thinking and in the life of our church. The truth of God's Word emboldened the hearts of our people. In God's sovereign goodness, that truth also served as an encouragement to many outside of our congregation. Like the previous sermon, this message also went viral. Every hour seemed to produce another thousand views.

TURNING MYSELF IN
Tuesday, February 16, 2021

Following the service, I was informed that the RCMP would be contacting me on Monday to make plans for me to turn myself in on Tuesday. Monday, February 15, was a holiday, and the justice of the peace (JP) would not be in session. That would have meant keeping me in a cell at the RCMP office in Spruce Grove, Alberta, from Sunday until Tuesday. The RCMP did not see that as necessary. They did not consider me a flight risk. The fact I would turn myself in on the morning of Tuesday, February 16, meant two more sleeps in my own bed.

On Tuesday morning, I spoke with the officer assigned to my case because I wanted to get a sense of what to expect. Should my wife drive me in? Would I be driving home later that day? Though the officer could not guarantee the outcome, he insinuated I could probably drive myself in. He believed I would be going home that day. We found out later he had never even considered the possibility that I would not sign my bail condition.

When I left that morning, I did so with a fair amount of optimism that I would be home that evening. Erin told me later she was not as optimistic. That was probably a grace for her. The drive took about forty-five minutes, and I drove with a sense of both peace and joy. I spoke with our associate pastor, Jacob Spenst, on the way in. I had already given him direction on what to do if I was taken into custody. He would take up my mantle and continue to shepherd the flock. My direction to the rest of the church leaders was that if Jacob was imprisoned, then they should comply with the government so that we would not lose all of the shepherds. Even so, the conviction to take a stand ran strong throughout our leadership.

When I arrived, there was already a faithful man from our church in the parking lot. He was there to pray. We did not interact for long, but it was a comfort to see him. I was then met by an officer, placed into an RCMP vehicle, and taken to the jail facility in back. I was asked to remove my jacket, shoes, overshirt, and belt. As I recall, I was patted down. Before long, I was in my cell awaiting my telecom appearance before the JP.

There was no clock in the cell, so it is difficult to get a sense for how much time was passing. I spent a while reading Paul's epistle to the Philippians and praying. At some point, I was served lunch, and then later took a nap. The cell was cold, there was little privacy, and the guard checked on me frequently to see how I was doing.

At some point that afternoon, it was time for my appearance before the JP. I was awakened from my nap, led out of my cell, and brought into a room. On the call was a JP (the first one), my lawyer, and the lawyer representing the Crown, who made it obvious she did not like me at all. That first hearing was adjourned to give time for my lawyer and the Crown to discuss a particular matter, but as I recall, it was during the second hearing that she rehearsed a grocery list of public health offenses supporting her contention that I was a danger to society and should be imprisoned.

Even though I believed both the law of God and highest law of the land would ultimately vindicate me, I still sensed the weight of my situation. At multiple points throughout my legal proceedings, the contrast between our church's position and the Crown's was stark. The Crown came across as dark, heavy-handed, merciless, and bleak. But when my lawyers spoke, we were characterized by truth, liberty, rationality, and sound judgment.

It occurred to me that the way the law was being used against me is similar to what will happen to those who go into the final judgment without Christ. This caused me to both grieve for those who reject Christ and to rejoice in the forgiveness of my sin. A person who is justified by grace alone, through faith alone, in Christ alone, will never experience the weight of God's moral law like that. "How blessed is he whose transgression is forgiven, whose sin is covered!" (Psalm 32:1).

Though the Crown wanted me imprisoned, the JP (the second one) signaled early in the proceedings that he did not think prison time was warranted. However, he indicated that though I would be released, it would not be without conditions. I would be required to comply with all existing health orders. At that point, the question was this: Would I be released and given that condition, or would my release be conditioned on my agreeing to comply? There is a difference. One would not require any commitment on my part to comply, while the other would. If it were the latter of the two, I was already settled on not signing those terms.

When the paperwork arrived, the officer who was with me already knew what I intended to do. He knew the dilemma I was in. When he read the condition, he said, "Looks like the decision has already been made for you." To be released, I would have to agree to abide by the condition.

Here is the predicament I was in: If I agreed to abide by the condition, then I would either singlehandedly and unilaterally force the church into compliance or resolve to stay at home while the church continued to gather. Neither was an option for me. I was not going to keep the Lord's people from their means of grace, and I was not going to be a coward and stay at home while GraceLife gathered. I certainly was not going to agree to a condition that I knew I would violate. Not only would that compromise my integrity, but it would also exponentially increase the legal trouble I was in. As I understood it, breaching a bail condition was immediately a criminal offence.

Not signing was not the hard part. The hard part was dealing with the implications of not signing. Though I had never been in trouble with the law before, I somehow knew from my childhood what it would feel like to be imprisoned. It felt exactly the way I thought it would. I was permitted to call James Kitchen at that point. I wept on the phone with him. After telling him what happened, he comforted me, prayed for me, and outlined what would happen legally in the days ahead. From there, after getting myself together, I called my family and broke the news to them.

BEING SHACKLED

In the middle of the night, an officer came to get me. He had been instructed to fingerprint me and take my mug shot. I did not feel at all comfortable with that. I kept asking the officer why that was even necessary. After all, I could have been released by then. I was there of my own volition. He simply said, "I'm just following orders." He told me if I was not convicted, then the mug shot would be removed from the system. But I had my doubts.

Because I would not sign, I had a hearing first thing the next morning in a provincial court. A different officer came to get me, cuffed me, and shackled me. I guess I had suddenly become a flight risk. He said it was protocol; in hindsight, I think it was all an effort to get me to crack and sign the condition. More on that later.

When I got to the provincial court, they did not know what to do with me. Not signing one's release condition is not typical. I was placed in a holding cell until my hearing. While there, I was able to share the gospel with one of the court officers. That encounter encouraged my heart as I considered the opportunities for the glory of Christ and the gospel that would result from my stand.

The hearing was uneventful. It essentially sealed my fate with respect to being transferred to the Edmonton Remand Centre, and a date was set for a future court hearing. As I was being led out of the building, I recognized a vehicle that pulled up. It was one of our elders-in-development. We could not interact for more than a moment, but he told me he loved me, and I reciprocated. Then as I was driven out of the parking lot, I saw another man from our church—the same man who had been praying for me when I initially turned myself in. He was walking on the sidewalk as he prayed. That brought tears to my eyes.

CHAPTER 9

TRUSTING GOD
FROM BEHIND BARS

James Coates

rior to being taken to Remand, I was brought back to the RCMP headquarters. I was permitted to use the phone, and I called Erin first. She was on the road driving to my location. As we talked, I came undone. In that moment, she exhorted me with strong conviction. Her steadfastness reminded me how precious a godly and supportive wife in ministry is. She helped me pull myself together. After that, I called James Kitchen. Then, I was transferred to Remand.

On the way there, the officer had the radio on, and my situation was already getting lots of attention. It was rather surreal. When we arrived, I was uncuffed and unshackled, and brought into an initial intake room. Two other individuals were also there. What you are being brought in for is of interest at that point. I told them I was a pastor and had violated the Public Health Act by conducting worship services. They thought that was ridiculous. Then one of them asked me to pray for him.

From there, I was transferred to a holding cell. I was given a cell to myself, apparently for my protection. There were multiple steps to being processed, and at each step, a guard would come get me, complete that step, and return me to my cell. The guards already knew who I was and why I was there, and they too thought my arrest was ridiculous. These were the first signs of support I received from the guards.

Being processed involves some unusual steps. For example, I had to remove the shoelaces from my shoes. This is done to prevent inmates from hanging themselves. Another part of the process involved a strip search by a guard responsible to make sure no drugs or weapons are brought into the facility.

After I had gone through most of the steps, I was placed in a holding cell with a few other inmates. One was on the floor sleeping and appeared to be detoxing from narcotics. He later became my first cellmate for a couple days. The others in the holding cell were talking, and their language was colorful. When they found out why I was there, one of them told me I would be fine. I do not recall what prompted him to say this. Though it might seem strange, I found a degree of comfort in his words.

Before long, we were transferred to our first pod and cell. Each pod consisted of a main floor with cells, as well as two additional levels of cells. When we arrived at our pod, the guard said, "Wonderful! Three criminals fresh off the street!" It is difficult to put into words how that sounded to me. I had an opportunity shortly thereafter to ask him if he knew why I was there. As he reached for my file, I told him I was a pastor. He could have blown me off and cussed me out, but he did not. Later, when I was back in my cell, he spoke over the intercom, and said, "Hey, preacher, you want some paper and a pen?" I said, "Sure!" He said, "John Bunyan did some of his best work in prison." It was another moment in which the Lord ministered grace to my heart.

We were under quarantine for what amounted to about fifteen days. While on quarantine, we were permitted two fifteen-minute exercises per day. That meant spending nearly twenty-four hours in a cell each day. One day I went almost twenty-four hours between exercises.

One of the unexpected surprises in prison was that we had access to four radio stations. One of the stations was talk radio that provided a news loop every thirty minutes. I was mentioned on that news loop often. In fact, we left the radio on throughout that first night, and there were multiple times when I heard excerpts from the previous Sunday's sermon. I was surprised by how much attention our church's situation was getting.

My first cellmate did a lot of sleeping. He slept day and night and awoke only to eat, use the bathroom, and take his exercise time, although sometimes he would even sleep through that. We shared the cell for only a couple of days. Due to the media attention I was getting, I was placed under administrative watch. There was concern that one of the other inmates might harm me. That meant I had to take my two fifteen-minute exercises on my own. It also meant my cellmate was removed from my cell, but not before I had shared the gospel with him.

Exercise was critical to having any meaningful connection to the outside world. I spent virtually every exercise talking to Erin. Those conversations were a lifeline, and she would fill me in on the impact my imprisonment was having—which was beyond anything that we had anticipated. The most memorable encouragement came from Pastor John MacArthur. Erin played an audio recording of a message he had sent to her. That put a fresh wind in my sail.

One exercise is particularly memorable. My first Sunday in jail, I received my fifteen minutes just prior to that morning's service. I called my wife and spoke to her for a few minutes. Then she let me speak to Pastor Jacob. He was in his first few months of ministry and was about to get into the pulpit and preach not knowing what would happen next. None of us did. It was conceivable that he might suffer the same fate I had. So I told him what I sometimes tell myself before a difficult sermon: "You have one thing to do. Preach and die." This is a way of saying you have one job to do: Preach the Word, and let the chips fall where they may. He got into the pulpit that morning and preached with courage and conviction. He essentially said, "You can take me away and there will be another, and then another, and then another." It was enough to put steel in your spine.

During the first few days, a lot of people came to visit me. Within the first day or two, I was also visited by one of the chaplains. He gave me a Bible and lots of literature. He also answered all my questions and equipped me with what to expect about life in prison. Another chaplain came to see me as well. During the first visit, he was as supportive as he could be without knowing whether I was the real deal. But by the second visit, he was even more supportive and knew why I was doing what I was. There was also a guard who knew people from our church. In the early going, these kinds of visits were a regular occurrence.

It did not take long to realize that those who ran the prison did not want me there. Within the first week, I was called out of my cell by three guards who were higher up the food chain. They said to me, "You understand that you do not need to be here, right?" All I had to do was say the word, and my release papers would have been processed. They could not understand why I would not sign the condition form.

In addition, I received a phone call from a professing Christian member of parliament. I suspect the premier of Alberta put him up to it. He spent the entire twenty-minute phone call attempting to persuade me, from Scripture, that I was doing the wrong thing. A side note here: during a call, you are notified when you have only a minute remaining. As it turned out, there was no goodbye at the end of this phone call because the parliamentarian spent the entire final minute hitting me from every angle, imploring me to sign the condition form. On another occasion, a guard approached me with a request from the premier himself. The request asked me to call a member of clergy. I gather I was supposed to contact him so he could persuade me to sign. It seemed unthinkable to them that I would not be willing to do so.

My wife later spoke with someone who works at Remand. According to this person, the "administrative watch" arrangement was made up in an effort to get me to crack. This person alleged that there was a note on my file encouraging regular visits in an attempt to persuade me to sign my condition form. My isolation and extended periods without exercise were apparently part of a ploy to weaken my resolve.

Prior to my transition from quarantine into general population, I found out someone had meddled with my file. My marital status was changed from married to common law, and my religion from either Christian or Baptist to Christian Science. Nothing has ever come of that, but it would seem that was done with the intent of discrediting me at some point. It certainly upped the ante on the battle for my mind.

One of the benefits of realizing I was not wanted at Remand was what it meant for our associate pastor, Pastor Jacob, and Pastor Tim Stephens (a fellow minister in Alberta who opened his congregation, Fairview Baptist Church). I remember saying to Pastor Jacob on either the first or second Sunday of my imprisonment, "They do not want you here." What's more, I was fairly certain my being there would keep Jacob and Tim out. It was my imprisonment that settled things for Fairview Baptist Church. They were open and not being shy about it. As I understand it, Pastor Tim contacted other pastors with a view toward building a coalition of churches that would be open and stand together. While I was in prison, I believe that number reached about twenty churches.

In prison, the battle for the mind is significant. You are isolated, disconnected from the outside world, and experiencing a completely different reality than normal. One of the biggest battles I remember involved my transition from quarantine to general pop-ulation. One of the advantages of being in quarantine is that it eases you into prison culture. It also provides a measure of protection. As the time for moving me to general population drew closer, I had a couple of encounters with people that sowed seeds of fear in my heart.

As noted above, we had access to radio in the prison. During this time, the media was subtly insinuating that I was a white suprem-acist. Nothing could be further from the truth. But one of the inmates, after figuring out who I was, came to my cell door and warned me that I would be unsafe once out of quarantine. This put me into a serious tailspin of anxiety—enough so that it was disrupt-ing my resolve and clarity of conviction. I knew I needed to pray. About a minute into that prayer, the first chaplain who had visited me earlier showed up. It was like God sending an angel to Daniel. He put my mind at ease. He had his finger on the pulse of the prison and knew the culture well. He said I had nothing to worry about, and he was right.

The support I received from the inmates was virtually unan-imous, and the very day I was transferred to general population, they began to seek me out. It is amazing how fast word travels in prison. Inmates on their exercise time would come to me for help and I would speak to them through the cell door. The first gentle-man who came to me had lost his five-year-old son in a fire. That led him to turn his back on God. It was a challenging situation for me to be placed in. But by God's grace, I was able to express sorrow and compassion to him, and share the gospel. After all, God gave His own Son that we might believe in Him and have everlasting life. Opportunities to share the gospel and provide counsel arose on a regular basis.

I was also able to start a Bible study. An inmate in the cell next to me was a professing Christian. A lot of inmates are. He asked me if we could do a Bible study, and because prisoners are not permitted to be in another inmate's cell, we set up the study on the main floor. I sat down at a table with my Bible, and within about a minute the table would be full. I would have four or five other inmates listen to me teach from the Gospel of John. I taught them about the identity of Christ (both His deity and humanity), the necessity of the new birth, and even got into that glorious chapter on the Good Shepherd. I always had a captive audience.

One of the greatest fuels for my perseverance was receiving letters of support. They came from all over the world. Often they arrived together, in large stacks. The guards preferred it that way because it meant having to make fewer deliveries. Though the guards tasked with photocopying the letters before they were distributed to the inmates were no doubt less thrilled. As I understand it, they photocopied the letters to ensure drugs were not being smuggled into the building. Apparently they had to read the mail too. For that reason, the people who wrote to me were diligent to include the gospel in their letters.

GRACE UNDER FIRE

While in prison, Erin was my mouthpiece. She did many interviews. And she was able to articulate the theological justification for our stand in a compelling way. Some took exception to the fact that she was doing most of the interviews and wondered where our church leaders were. But as my wife, she was the one in demand, and she was well equipped to speak on my behalf. I would venture to say that her interview responses, in conjunction with my imprisonment, worked together to open many people's eyes. To a large extent, she was able to counter the false picture being painted of me by the mainstream media. There were unsaved members in my own extended family whose minds were changed after seeing her interviews. We were the perfect team.

The most significant interview she did was Tucker Carlson Tonight on Fox News.[28] It has had more than a million views on

YouTube alone. That interview likely reached multiple millions of people. It seemed to create a stir even before it was recorded. CTV News, a member of the mainstream media, would not allow Erin into their building to do the interview. This was after it had already been scheduled and the paperwork signed. As I understand it, that was an unusual development. But that interview seemed to move the dial on the government's desire to get me out of prison. It was recorded on Friday, March 12, 2021, and aired the following Thursday, on March 18. By the time it aired, there was already an agreement in place between my lawyers and the Crown for my release.

CHAPTER 10

THE UNDERGROUND
CHURCH OF CANADA

James Coates

A t this time, a second lawyer was added to my team. Leighton
Grey is a seasoned attorney who manages the courtroom
incredibly well, and is a strong advocate for constitutional
liberty. We had made attempts to remove the condition of my
release in court, but they had failed. Leighton then reached out to
the Crown to see if they would be willing to alter my bail condition
to a basic "keep the peace" arrangement. However, I would not have
agreed to that either. In layman's terms, to keep the peace is to keep
the law. But given the way the Public Health Act was being enforced,
holding a church service would put me in violation of that condition. As I said earlier, for a person to violate their bail condition esca-
lates things substantially.

Unexpectedly, the Crown came back with an offer that was even
better than that. And the timing is noteworthy. This happened in
the days following Erin's recording of the Tucker Carlson interview,
which had received public attention even before it was aired. In the

deal, the Crown offered to drop all the charges but one, so long as I pled guilty to a provincial offense in connection with breaching the undertaking of my initial arrest. The charge that remained would allow me to continue to contest the legitimacy of the Public Health Act in light of the Canadian Charter. It was an offer that conveyed to me that the government and Crown were taking my conviction, principle, and stand seriously.

Though the offer was compelling, I requested we counter with one in which I did not plead guilty to anything. The Crown refused. So, it was on me to decide whether to accept their offer. Did I like the idea of pleading guilty? No. But I would be pleading guilty to what I actually did, as illegitimate as the initial undertaking may have been, and I could return to my family and my flock. Had I rejected, it is possible I could have waited out the Crown long enough for all the charges to be dropped. But if I had done that, my stand would have shifted from a theological one to a political one. It would have gone from being Christ-centered to me-centered. So I agreed to plead guilty to the provincial offense and come away without a criminal record.

That was a challenging week. I was on the cusp of being released, yet things seemed to be happening so slowly. The agreement was in place. All that was left was to set a court date. Through sheer oversight, it was thought that the soonest available court date was Monday, March 22. Efforts were made to get me into a court in a different jurisdiction the Friday before, which was the day following the Tucker Carlson interview. But given the intensely public nature of my situation, that court refused to hold my hearing. By the time we learned that, we also discovered that the court where I was supposed to appear had been in session earlier that week. Had we known, we could have gotten in earlier. But in God's providence, He wanted me in prison for the weekend—maybe to ensure that the Tucker Carlson interview aired.

MY RELEASE

March 22, 2021

I was in court on the morning of Monday, March 22, appearing via livestream. Though it is highly unusual for a judge to reject a plea bargain, this judge seemed to want me to sweat it out a bit. He gave the impression he was not satisfied with the agreement on the basis that it was not in the best interests of the law. In the agreement, I would receive a $100 fine, and he was suggesting a harsher penalty might be in order. He also subtly suggested that penalty could include additional jail time. I suspect the judge was wanting to be difficult. I do not think he had any intention of standing in the way of the agreement. He adjourned the hearing, went to his chambers, and came back with a fine of $1,500. Increasing the fine was somewhat moot because the time I had spent in jail more than covered what the maximum fine could have been.

Prior to adjourning, the judge gave me what my lawyers called a tongue-lashing. In it, he described my actions as being inconsistent with my role as a shepherd. In his estimation, the call for a shepherd to protect his sheep necessitates shutting down the corporate gathering to protect them from the virus. The judge also suggested that the motivation for my stand was to establish myself as a political revolutionary. When I was given the opportunity to speak, I said the following:

> Well, your Honor, I would just convey that in light of the original undertaking, where I was presented with the condition of the undertaking, I was unable to sign that condition and would just want to indicate that my integrity and my word have been consistent throughout this entire time.
>
> I'm not here to make a statement. I realize that's the way society is going to parse out what's happening here. I'm

simply here in obedience to Jesus Christ, and it's my
obedience to Christ that has put me at odds with the
law at present.

The court is aware that I'm contesting the legitimacy of
that law, and so I think that my position is pretty clear,
but please make no mistake. This is not a statement that
I'm making to society. I'm not trying to make a point.
I'm not a political revolutionary. I have a responsibility
before God to shepherd the people entrusted to me. I
have a responsibility to be obedient to my Lord and Savior Jesus Christ, and it's simply that obedience that has
me here in this place.

My lawyers felt this seemed to quell the judge's impression of me
as a political revolutionary. When he rendered his verdict after the
adjournment, his disposition seemed somewhat different. It was a
blessing to be able to testify to the lordship of Christ in that moment.

After the hearing, I was taken back to my pod and my cell knowing I would be released later that day. I shared the news with my
cellmate and started to pack my stuff. Shortly thereafter, one of the
guards called to me through the intercom and told me I would be
leaving that afternoon, and that I should get ready. There was even
some excitement in his voice when he made the announcement.

It was hard not to anticipate what leaving the pod would be like.
Given the way the inmates had responded to me, it seemed plausi-
ble that it would be a moment to remember. Most of the inmates
knew I would be leaving that day. The news broadcasts had been
talking about my Monday court appearance over the weekend and
were already announcing my release.

I got a sense of what leaving would be like when one of the chaplains came to see me. A guard spoke over the intercom and called me
down to meet the chaplain. I was not sure what to do, so I grabbed
my bag so as to be ready to leave. There was an inmate I wanted to

connect with before leaving, so I ran a few cells down to tell him I would be praying for him. As I did that, there was already noise coming from the other cells around me. I think the inmates thought I was leaving right then. A guard hollered up to me on the third floor and said I was not leaving yet, and not to bring my bag. I returned my bag, and went down to spend some time with the chaplain.

It is hard to remember what we talked about. He was no doubt encouraging me to stay strong. We were not able to get a room for that discussion and were sitting at a table out in the open. While we were talking, a guard said, "Okay, Coates, you're leaving!" The chaplain and I stood, shook hands, and prayed together. I ran upstairs to my cell, grabbed my bag, and came back down. My floor was on exercise at the time, so I said goodbye to the guys. Then as I was walking to the door to exit the pod, there was a rumbling noise coming from the inmates who were in their cells. I stopped, turned around, and acknowledged them with my hand in the air. And the place shook. It was an incredible moment. I looked over at the guards to say goodbye to them, and I could tell even they were affected by what was happening. They said goodbye, and I was escorted out of the pod to be processed for release.

Unfortunately, the sweetness of that moment quickly subsided. In prison, you are essentially treated as property. So being processed both on the way in and on the way out is a rather dehumanizing experience. I was placed in a holding cell with other inmates who were leaving. There, I had to wait as the steps for my release were completed. The entire process takes about two hours. I called Erin to let her know it was time to come get me.

When I was finally free to leave the facility, I walked to a door and exited the building. My family was outside, waiting. As soon as I stepped out, I was embraced by Erin and our two boys. There is video footage of that available from Rebel News,[29] courtesy of a gentleman in our church. From there, our goal was to get to our vehicle without having to interact with the media.

As we got on the highway to head home, I broke down and wept. Even to this day, it is hard for me to put my finger on why. They were not tears of joy, but of grief. I had just been exposed to an aspect of our society that is both dark and corrupt. Man's fallen condition was on display in manifold ways. The tears I wept expressed what I was unable to say.

RETURNING TO LIFE AND MINISTRY
Late March 2021

It did not take long for things to get hectic. Once out of prison, I was inundated with media requests. One came from Danielle Smith, who was formerly involved in politics at the provincial level and is well known in our province. During my first week in prison while listening to the radio, I heard her grill our premier about my imprisonment. Needless to say, I was willing to appear on her program.

Danielle made the announcement on social media about my appearance on Friday, March 26. On Saturday, March 27, we received correspondence from AHS offering a virtual meeting to discuss the science behind COVID and AHS's lockdown measures. Receiving correspondence from AHS on Saturday was highly unusual, and I suspected Danielle's announcement triggered it. I believe they wanted to keep me silent.

In addition, AHS and the RCMP attempted to gain access to our facility on Sunday morning. This too seemed strange, because during the five weeks of my imprisonment, neither AHS nor the RCMP visited our property. They simply parked on the road at a distance. I received word of this a minute or two before the beginning of the service and had to go into the pulpit not knowing what their intentions were. In the end, two of our church leaders were able to keep them out. There is video footage of that interaction compliments of Rebel News.[30] Both men handled the situation phenomenally.

I had asked pastor Mike Hovland to preach that Sunday. He was formerly our associate pastor and had moved eight hours north to pastor a church plant in La Crete, Alberta. Mike played an important role in our stand. In fact, the week that I was imprisoned, he drove from La Crete to Edmonton to attend our elders meeting in person. His leadership at that stage was critical; Pastor Jacob had been in ministry for only four months. It was resurrection Sunday, and Mike preached a powerful sermon declaring the glorious truth that Jesus is seated in the heavenly places far above all rule and authority. The message put fire in my bones.

OUR BUILDING IS IMPRISONED

April 7, 2021

The following week, on Wednesday, April 7, I woke up with texts on my phone from our administrative assistant. He woke up to the sound of the alarm system going off at our church facility. When he checked the video footage, he could see AHS was changing our locks. Our building was now theirs and would be until we complied with their health orders. But they did not stop at changing the locks. They set up three rows of fencing around the building and enlisted security to provide twenty-four-hour onsite surveillance. That was both bizarre and completely unnecessary. Changing the locks would have sufficed.

As a result, our facility became ground zero in the fight for freedom between our church and our government. It looked like a scene from Communist China. Many of us went there to see what was going on. It was surreal. The RCMP was present. The media was present. There were onlookers present. Yet, in all that activity, there was peace and calm in the air. Though we might have had reason to be discouraged, I was eager to see what God would do. Our government was going toe-to-toe with the Lord Jesus Christ. That did not bode well for the government.

GOING UNDERGROUND
April 11, 2021

Some have wondered why we opted to go underground. Why not continue to meet out in the open? The primary motivation was to protect the owners of the locations where we were meeting. When the battle rages on your own turf, you assume all legal liability. But when it comes to using someone else's property, it is natural to want to protect them. Though each of the owners were willing to face the repercussions for hosting an illegal gathering on their property, we did all we could to avoid unnecessary legal exposure. In addition, meeting at undisclosed locations facilitated undistracted worship.

When AHS seized our facility, the pressing matter quickly became where we would gather on Sunday. We had several options. One was to meet on the property next to our facility. It is owned by a gentleman who attends our church. Another was to meet at the Legislature, a typical location for protests. But we received an offer late in the week to meet at a location that provided an enclosed structure and was large enough to accommodate our church body. We met there, and both the worship and fellowship were sweet.

While we were there, unknown to us, a protest was taking place at our facility. Though it was predominantly peaceful, tensions escalated at one point and some people attempted to take down the outermost perimeter of fencing. The aftermath of that event was rather chaotic. Some tried to pin the protest on us. But as the recorded service demonstrates, we were together at a different and undisclosed location, doing what we had always done: worshipping our Lord and Savior, Jesus Christ.

Though we had gone 37 weeks in our facility without a single incident of COVID, it hit us hard in the days following that Sunday. For a few weeks, it seemed like many of our people became sick. My family came down with COVID too. But we see that as a blessing, as it enabled our congregation to develop herd immunity. Furthermore, for this to happen to our congregation when it did was providential.

From then onward, we made use of multiple undisclosed locations, most of which had us entirely outdoors. We employed a two-step process for securing each site. Over time, we also developed a culture of secrecy among the congregation to ensure our location would not be compromised. Not only was this practice for what could become the norm in our country, it was critical in light of an underhanded court order.

THE COURT ORDER
May 2021

On May 6, AHS secured a court order against a restaurant not far from our church. But the order was written so broadly that it implicated any public gathering deemed out of compliance. Once served in advance with this court order, anyone later hosting an illegal gathering would be arrested and found in contempt of court. The penalty for contempt of court comes with up to a two-year prison sentence.

On Sunday, May 9, we were in a certain location for the second week in a row. Following that service, a number of reports came to our attention that unmarked police vehicles had been seen in the area. We sensed this meant we needed to meet in a different location the following Sunday. Also on that Sunday, the Calgary Police attempted to serve Pastor Tim Stephens with the court order, but accidently served someone else. That suggested they were intending to use the court order against us.

On Thursday, May 13, the Justice Center for Constitutional Freedoms (JCCF) successfully argued in court that the language of the order needed to be modified to limit it to the original establishment.[31] But even though AHS agreed to the amendment, they were moving forward as though nothing had changed.[32] It was clear that AHS was manipulating the system to suit their heavy-handed agenda.

Because we had agreed to meet at an entirely new location the following Sunday, I drove there feeling less weight than usual on my shoulders. However, that quickly changed upon arrival. First, a number of people were having trouble finding the location. That resulted in an unusual amount of traffic being rerouted from the same spot. Second, the vehicle in front of me turned early into a residential property. I followed, and another car followed me. That meant three vehicles were now doing a U-turn on a rural residential property. Third, the road we had to take to get to the location made us highly visible. We were practically waving at neighbors on the way in. Not exactly covert. Making matters worse, on the side of the road sat a couple in their golf cart. They had a mobile phone in hand and did not look happy. By the time we arrived at the correct location, I was feeling a lot of pressure. At this time, we were not entirely clear on whether we had to be served with the court order before being arrested.

Thankfully, one of our members approached the couple during all the confusion and said we were a church, and that if they were going to call the police, to please let us know. When they found out we were a church, they were delighted. When they found out we were GraceLife Church, their delight increased! They told us they would take care of the situation with all the neighbors. Though that was good news for us, that location was likely compromised going forward.

Our time together that Sunday was phenomenal—that is, until I left the property and fired up my mobile device. As the texts rolled in, I learned that the RCMP had been at the other location with two unmarked minivans and a K-9 unit. I was almost certain that had we met at that location, we would have been served with the court order and our entire leadership team would have been arrested following the service. I also found out Pastor Tim had been arrested and taken into custody. Though the Calgary Police had failed to serve him with the court order the week before, they arrested him anyway. Thankfully, his arrest was tossed in court given that he had not first been served with the order.

Pastor Tim was later served with the same court order on Saturday, June 5. This was despite the fact the court order only applied to a specific establishment, and not to churches. Though we had received word that the RCMP would not enforce that court order, Calgary Police Services apparently would. At that point, Tim had to decide whether Fairview Baptist Church would still meet or not. In the end, he courageously decided to press on, and they met that Sunday.

I called Pastor Tim on the way home from our gathering that Sunday to find out what had happened. They, too, had been locked out of their building and were meeting outside. But Fairview was able to meet without incident, and Tim was home with his family later that day. They met again the following Sunday, on June 13, and Tim was arrested Monday afternoon.[33] It was a shocking turn of events. First, the court order should not have been used against him. Second, the province would be lifting the lockdowns in less than three weeks. He spent 17 nights in jail. I was now able to appreciate what he went through because of my imprisonment. It was excruciating. It is difficult to enjoy any aspect of life knowing your brother is unjustly incarcerated.

ALBERTA REMOVES RESTRICTIONS
July 1, 2021

On Thursday, July 1, our province removed nearly all the lockdown restrictions. Our building was returned to us. Fairview's building was returned to them. Pastor Tim was released from prison. We were back in our respective facilities to worship on Sunday, July 4.

Though we had already been gathering in the months prior, and though some found it difficult to rejoice in receiving back our facility, that Sunday was glorious. God had carried us through an immeasurably difficult season. We had seen His hand of faithfulness.

It is unlikely the battle is over. Government totalitarianism not only remains on the rise in Canada, it seems to be on the rise globally. Regardless of what the future holds, God will always be faithful. His faithfulness in the past will be critical to enduring the tribulations of the present. May He keep us faithful, all the way to the end, for His glory and the good of His people.

In all these matters, we continue to trust the One who holds the future in His hands. He declares the end from the beginning, and His perfect purposes are never thwarted (Job 42:2). Our courage to stand firm comes from knowing He is with us (Hebrews 13:5-6). Our prayer is that others will be strengthened to take a bold and biblical stand for Christ and His church. We seek to remain steadfast by God's grace and for His glory. And so we echo the words of Paul from Romans 11:33-36:

> Oh, the depth of the riches both of the wisdom and knowledge of God! How unsearchable are His judgments and unfathomable His ways! For who has known the mind of the Lord, or who became His counselor? Or who has first given to Him that it might be paid back to him again? For from Him and through Him and to Him are all things. To Him be the glory forever. Amen.

PART 2

OUR STAND

CHAPTER 11

FIVE BIBLICAL
PRINCIPLES

Nathan Busenitz

F
ive centuries ago, in 1521, the Protestant Reformer Martin Luther was summoned to appear before Charles V, the
emperor of the Holy Roman Empire and the most powerful monarch in Europe. Luther had been excommunicated from
the Roman Catholic Church a few months prior. He was charged
with heresy for his vocal opposition to theological error and religious corruption in the church. If convicted, Luther would likely
be sentenced to death.

The imperial council, known as a diet, met in the city of Worms,
located in modern-day Germany. Luther arrived on April 16, 1521,
and appeared before the assembly the following day at 4:00 in the
afternoon. A stack of his books was presented, and he was asked if
he would recant the alleged heresies they contained. Recognizing
what was at stake and wanting to give a careful answer, the German
Reformer asked for more time. He was given twenty-four hours.

The following day, on April 18, 1521, Luther boldly declared before
the council that he would not recant his views. Famously, he said,
"Unless I am convinced by Scripture and plain reason—I do not

accept the authority of the popes and councils, for they have contra-
dicted each other—my conscience is captive to the Word of God. I
cannot, and I will not recant anything for to go against conscience
is neither right nor safe. God help me. Amen."[34] Instead of complying and falling in line, he boldly defied those in authority over him,
including the emperor himself.

Luther's courage was grounded in conviction, and that conviction was anchored in his commitment to the supreme authority
of Christ and His Word. His conscience was bound to the Word
of God. Its authority superseded that of popes, councils, and even
emperors. Despite the possibility of incarceration or execution,
Luther did not waver before the most powerful monarch of his day.
He remained true to his biblical convictions, refused to violate his
conscience, and entrusted himself to the Lord.

As those who hold to the Protestant principle of *sola Scriptura*,
that Scripture alone is our final authority for faith and practice, we
are also bound to follow the Word of God. When navigating com-
plex situations, like how to respond to government restrictions
during a global pandemic, it is helpful to begin by identifying the
relevant biblical principles. These principles inform the conscience,
establish convictions, and provide a God-honoring grid for real-
time decision making.

In this chapter, we will survey five biblical principles regarding
the believer's response to and relationship with the government. The
chapter is arranged with numbered subpoints under each principle
that provide additional explanation and clarity. Though not exhaus-
tive, it is hoped this information will provide readers with a biblical
starting point for thinking through these important issues.

PRINCIPLE 1: SUPREME ALLEGIANCE

Why would the elders of Grace Community Church and
GraceLife Edmonton take the stand they did? The answer begins

with the conviction that Christ is the head of the church. As the Lord of His people, He is our highest authority. Our ultimate allegiance is to Him. When God and government collide, we must obey Christ rather than men (Acts 5:29).

1. The Christian worldview is founded on a commitment to the lordship of Jesus Christ (Romans 10:9). To be a Christian is to be a follower of Jesus Christ. We view our lives as an act of worship to Him, seeking to honor and please Him in all we do (Romans 12:1; 2 Corinthians 5:9).

2. We recognize that Jesus is Lord over (a) all creation (Acts 10:36), (b) all nations (Daniel 7:14; Romans 10:12), (c) the church (Ephesians 1:19-23), and (d) the life of each individual believer (Romans 14:7-9). One day, His supremacy will be confessed by every tongue as every knee bows in subjection to Him (Philippians 2:9-11).

3. Because the Lord Jesus is our highest authority, we submit to Him first and foremost. Our allegiance to Him surpasses and trumps our allegiance to any lower authority. When Peter and the apostles were commanded by the religious authorities of Israel to stop preaching about Jesus, they refused to comply. They were compelled to obey Christ over any earthly authority. As Luke records in Acts 4:18-20: "When they [the religious leaders] had summoned them, they commanded them not to speak or teach at all in the name of Jesus. But Peter and John answered and said to them, 'Whether it is right in the sight of God to give heed to you rather than to God, you be the judge; for we cannot stop speaking about what we have seen and heard.'"

4. Our allegiance to Christ is underscored by the reality that we are first and foremost citizens of heaven (Philippians 3:20-21). In this world, we are sojourners and strangers (Hebrews 11:13; 1 Peter 2:11). Our heavenly citizenship informs our perspective regarding the temporary things of this world (cf. 1 John 2:16-17).

5. One day, we will give an account to Christ (Romans 14:12; 2 Corinthians 5:10). He is both our highest authority and our

ultimate accountability. He is the judge of all men (John 5:25-27), and the Lord who examines His church (Revelation 2–3). His measure of success is faithfulness to Him (Matthew 25:21). Any suffering or persecution we experience in this life is but a blip compared to the eternal reward that awaits those who are faithful to Him (2 Corinthians 4:17).

6. Because our supreme allegiance belongs to Christ, His Word serves as our highest authority (see Matthew 7:26; John 10:27; Colossians 3:16). Our response to governing officials flows from the truth of divine revelation, which is found on the pages of Scripture.

7. As Christians, we demonstrate our love for Him through our obedience to Him (John 14:15; 15:14). When we submit to governing authorities, we do so out of obedience to Christ. Conversely, if obedience to our Lord requires us not to comply with a government mandate or injunction, we must obey God rather than men (Acts 5:29).

PRINCIPLE 2: SOVEREIGN APPOINTMENT

We recognize that all human authority is delegated by God, who is sovereign over all rulers and kingdoms. He has defined the proper role of government in His Word. Passages like Romans 13 define God's intention for governing authorities. When those in government exceed the God-given limits of their authority, they do so in violation of the One who grants their authority to them.

1. God is the supreme authority over the entire universe. No other authority exists without His express permission and sovereign determination (Psalms 10:16; 22:28; 47:8; 1 Timothy 1:17). As Daniel 4:32 explains, "The Most High is ruler over the realm of mankind and bestows it on whomever He wishes."

2. After creating the universe, God gave human beings authority to rule over the earth (Genesis 1:26-30; 2:15). He also gave them the prerogative to exercise capital punishment (Genesis 9:6).

These divine ordinances provide the basis for human government (Romans 13:1-7).

3. Every human government is given its authority by God (Daniel 2:37, 44; 4:25; 5:21; 7:27). He establishes the temporal and geographical extent of every kingdom, nation, and human governing authority (Acts 17:26; cf. Proverbs 21:1).

4. Those in government are accountable to God for how they exercise the authority He has given to them (Romans 13:6). God's dealing with Nebuchadnezzar in Daniel 4 provides a vivid example of this principle. The most powerful ruler in the world at the time, Nebuchadnezzar was dramatically humiliated so that he would learn his rightful place under God's authority.

5. God has designed the proper role for government. That role primarily consists of promoting good and protecting the righteous, while preventing evil and punishing the wicked (Romans 13:1-6). Those rulers who govern well, upholding biblical morality and serving their people, are applauded by Scripture (2 Kings 22:2; 2 Chronicles 25:2). Conversely, those rulers who lead their people into wickedness are condemned (1 Kings 15:26; 2 Kings 23:37).

6. The government has the right to collect taxes to accomplish its God-given purpose. Christians are called to pay their taxes (Romans 13:6-7). Paying taxes is not dependent on whether the government operates according to biblical principles. Jesus instructed His followers to pay their taxes, even to the pagan Roman government (Matthew 22:21).

7. When a government abuses its power, using its authority in ways that are outside of its God-designed purpose, it does so in violation of God's law. Those in positions of civil authority are not above the law of God.

8. Citizens suffer when those in power exercise their authority in reckless or corrupt ways (Proverbs 29:2, 4). Such situations can be especially challenging for believers as they attempt to live in a way that honors the Lord. Even so, believers are to trust the Lord to

make things right, and to bring to judgment the actions of wicked rulers (Psalm 11:1-7; Romans 12:14-21).

9. One day, God will establish the perfect government, under the reign of His Son, the Lord Jesus Christ (Daniel 7:13-14). Believers look forward to the day when the Lord returns (1 Thessalonians 1:10; Titus 2:11-14). He will establish His kingdom and will reign as the perfect King (Revelation 20:1-6). His government will fulfill all that God designed government to be and to do.

PRINCIPLE 3: SECULAR ANIMOSITY

As Christians, we should expect to suffer at the hands of those who are part of the world. That includes persecution from non-Christian government officials. At some point, faithfulness to Christ will result in hostility from unbelievers, including from those in positions of civil authority.

1. Though God designed government to promote and protect good, and to prevent and punish evil, fallen human governments often do the opposite. In so doing, they reflect the corruption and antagonism of the world (Romans 1:18-32). For His part, God laughs at those who oppose Him, as if they could successfully thwart His plans and purposes (Psalm 2:1-12).

2. Throughout human history, hostile governments have been a primary persecutor of the people of God. The Pharaohs of Egypt enslaved and subjugated the Israelites. The kings of Israel and Judah often persecuted the prophets. Herod executed James and imprisoned Peter (Acts 12:1-3). Roman emperors, like Nero, violently persecuted the early church. In the end, the Antichrist will seek to kill God's people during the Great Tribulation (Revelation 13:7-8).

3. The Lord Jesus warned His followers they would be mistreated and persecuted by hostile government authorities (Matthew 10:16-20; Luke 12:8-12). In John 15:18-21, He told them, "If the world hates you, you know that it has hated Me before it hated you. If you

were of the world, the world would love its own; but because you are not of the world, but I chose you out of the world, because of this the world hates you. Remember the word that I said to you, 'A slave is not greater than his master.' If they persecuted Me, they will also persecute you; if they kept My word, they will keep yours also. But all these things they will do to you for My name's sake, because they do not know the One who sent Me."

4. Jesus Himself was falsely accused, unjustly tried, and finally crucified by wicked governing officials. Despite His innocence, He was treated as if He were a common criminal (Isaiah 53:9; Luke 24:32) and was executed as an enemy of the state (cf. John 19:12).

5. Though Jesus was severely mistreated, He did not respond with anger, malice, violence, or vengeance. He exemplified long-suffering, patience, and silence in His suffering (Isaiah 53:7). In this, He left us an example to follow (1 Peter 2:21-25).

6. Believers should expect to be persecuted by those in authority not because of any wrongdoing, but simply for their faithfulness to Christ. When they suffer in that sense, they are blessed. The apostle Peter highlighted that point in 1 Peter 4:14-16: "If you are reviled for the name of Christ, you are blessed, because the Spirit of glory and of God rests on you. Make sure that none of you suffers as a murderer, or thief, or evildoer, or a troublesome meddler; but if anyone suffers as a Christian, he is not to be ashamed, but is to glorify God in this name."

7. Church history is filled with examples of those who suffered and died for the sake of Christ. Early on, the apostles were punished for their allegiance to Jesus. They rejoiced that they had been counted worthy to suffer for His name's sake (Acts 5:40-42).

8. Passages like Romans 13:1-7 and 1 Peter 2:13-17 should be interpreted against the backdrop of persecution and suffering, because that is the context in which they were written (see Romans 12:14-21; 1 Peter 3:13-18). The main takeaway from those passages is that even when they are persecuted, believers are still commanded to

maintain an attitude of submission toward those in authority. Christians do not respond with vengeance or violence, but with kindness, longsuffering, respect, and grace.

PRINCIPLE 4: A SUBMISSIVE ATTITUDE

As a rule, believers are to obey those in authority over them. However, there will be times when they are not able to comply because they must obey God (Acts 5:29). Even when compliance is not possible, believers are still commanded to exhibit an attitude of respect and grace. They are not to respond with vitriol, violence, or vengeance.

1. There are four key New Testament passages that directly address the Christian's response to government: Romans 13:1-7, 1 Timothy 2:1-8, Titus 3:1-2, and 1 Peter 2:13-17. These passages are consistent in instructing believers to be exemplary citizens who submit to governing officials in civil matters.

2. These passages should be interpreted in light of the theological principles that have already been established. For example, we understand our allegiance to Christ supersedes our obligation to obey human rulers. When God and government collide, we must obey God rather than men (Acts 5:29).

3. These passages should also be understood in light of the men who wrote them. Their meaning must be consistent with the examples of their authors. Peter openly refused to stop preaching when ordered to do so by the rulers of Israel (Acts 4:19-20; 5:27-32). He also escaped from prison on two separate occasions (Acts 5, 12). Doing so not only broke the law, it also resulted in the deaths of the soldiers who had been guarding him (Acts 12:19). Paul evaded civil authorities by escaping from Damascus in a basket (Acts 9:23-25). He refused to comply when the Philippian magistrates asked him to leave the city secretly after they had mistreated him despite his Roman citizenship (Acts 16:35-40). On multiple occasions, he was

arrested and either punished or incarcerated (2 Corinthians 11:23-25; Ephesians 6:20; Philippians 1:7; Hebrews 13:3, 23) because he would not stop proclaiming the gospel. Both Peter and Paul were ultimately executed as enemies of the state under the imperial persecution of Nero. Their examples demonstrate it is not inherently wrong to be at odds with the government, depending on the reason for it.

4. These passages should be understood within their immediate contexts. When we consider Romans 13, for example, we might make a number of key observations (outlined below). For example, in keeping with a peaceful response to one's enemies (Romans 12:14-21), believers are to be submissive to governing authorities. Within the realm of civil matters, believers are to seek to obey their rulers. In Romans 13:1, Paul states the matter plainly: "Every person is to be in subjection to the governing authorities." The apostle makes this same point in Titus 3:1-2.

5. The reason believers submit to civil authority is because that authority is ordained by God. In being subject to human rulers, they are submitting themselves to God, who sovereignly ordained those rulers. As Paul writes, "There is no authority except from God, and those which exist are established by God" (Romans 13:1).

6. When people respond to civil authority with an unsubmissive attitude, ultimately, they are resisting the authority of God. They will reap the consequences of their disobedience, because God has given government the right to punish (and even execute) those who rebel. Romans 13:2 relates this point clearly: "Whoever resists authority has opposed the ordinance of God; and they who have opposed will receive condemnation upon themselves."

7. God designed governments to uphold good and repel evil within society. When a government is functioning properly, it protects those who do good and punishes those who do evil. In this way, a government functions as a servant of God. Paul explains this point in Romans 13:3-4: "Rulers are not a cause of fear for good behavior,

but for evil. Do you want to have no fear of authority? Do what is good and you will have praise from the same; for it is a minister of God to you for good. But if you do what is evil, be afraid; for it does not bear the sword for nothing; for it is a minister of God, an avenger who brings wrath on the one who practices evil."

8. By being subject to civil authority, believers can avoid potential punishment while also maintaining a clear conscience before the Lord. Hence, Paul writes, "Therefore it is necessary to be in subjection, not only because of wrath, but also for conscience' sake" (Romans 13:5).

9. It is right (and necessary) for believers to pay taxes so that civil authorities can have the resources necessary to carry out their God-given responsibilities. The text of Romans 13 makes this point explicit: "Because of this you also pay taxes, for rulers are servants of God, devoting themselves to this very thing" (Romans 13:6).

10. Believers are to render to civil authorities the honor, deference, and taxes that are rightly due to them (cf. 1 Peter 2:17). Paul's words may have shocked the believers in Rome, especially during the reign of a wicked emperor like Nero. Nonetheless, Paul's instruction is clear: "Render to all what is due them: tax to whom tax *is* due; custom to whom custom; fear to whom fear; honor to whom honor" (Romans 13:7).

11. The good behavior that characterizes believers is grounded not in human legislation but in God's law. That truth recognizes the priority of God's law over the laws of civil governments. Paul makes this point implicitly in Romans 13:8-10, which flows from his discussion about how to honor governing authorities: "Owe nothing to anyone except to love one another; for he who loves his neighbor has fulfilled the law. For this, 'You shall not commit adultery, you shall not murder, you shall not steal, you shall not covet,' and if there is any other commandment, it is summed up in this saying, 'You shall love your neighbor as yourself.' Love does no wrong to a neighbor; therefore love is the fulfillment of the law."

12. When believers react without violence, but in ways marked by love and righteousness, they shine like a bright light in a dark world (Matthew 5:12-16). This is consistent with the kind of behavior that ought to characterize them as followers of Jesus (Romans 13:11-13). This example serves as a witness to unbelievers who are watching.

13. Believers are also instructed to pray for those in positions of authority. First Timothy 2:1-2 emphasizes this point. Paul writes, "First of all, then, I urge that entreaties and prayers, petitions and thanksgivings, be made on behalf of all men, for kings and all who are in authority, so that we may lead a tranquil and quiet life in all godliness and dignity."

14. The Lord Jesus provides the perfect example for how we are to conduct ourselves, both in relationship to an unbelieving culture and in relationship to the government. Paul instructs his readers to "put on the Lord Jesus Christ" (Romans 13:14), and Peter states that Christ is the example believers should follow (1 Peter 2:21-25).

15. Significantly, Jesus did not always comply with the restrictions or regulations imposed by local governing authorities.

a. For example, in contradiction to the Pharisees, Jesus ignored the nonbiblical regulations they had added to the Sabbath (Mark 3:1-6). He also permitted His disciples to disregard certain extrabiblical regulations, like ceremonial hand washings (Mark 7:1-13).

b. In contradiction to the Sadducees (who controlled the temple), Jesus cleansed the temple on two separate occasions (John 2:13-22; 21:12-17). Due to Jesus' popularity, the high priest regarded Him as a public enemy who needed to be executed (John 11:47-53).

c. On multiple occasions, Jesus publicly rebuked the leaders of Israel for being corrupt (cf. Matthew

23:13-29). His bold response to their leadership and His willingness to break their rabbinic rules resulted in their anger and hostility toward Jesus (cf. Luke 6:11).

  d. At times, Jesus hid Himself to avoid capture by His enemies (John 8:59). He evaded Herod even though Herod wanted to see Him (Luke 9:9). But once arrested, He did not resist, but instead, suffered to the point of death (John 18:11, 36).

16. These examples from the life of our Lord are instructive for our understanding of how to submit to governing authorities (Romans 13:14; 1 Corinthians 11:1; 1 Peter 2:21-25). Jesus did not comply with regulations that were contrary to God's law, or that contributed to the corrupt legalism of first-century religious practice (Mark 7:1-14).

For additional helpful thoughts on Romans 13, especially as it relates to the God-ordained role for government, see chapter 14 in this book.

PRINCIPLE 5: SPHERES OF AUTHORITY

While believers are called to submit to human rulers, they also recognize that some matters fall outside the jurisdiction of civil authority. Historically, believers have identified worship practices, doctrinal convictions, and church polity as matters that are not subject to the authority of the state. The term *polity* refers to the leadership and organizational structure of the church. These matters fall under the jurisdiction of the shepherds (pastors and elders) of each local congregation as they determine how best to lead and care for their flock.

1. Our perfect example, the Lord Jesus, designated different spheres of authority when He taught His disciples to render to Caesar the things that are Caesar's, and to God the things that are God's

(Matthew 22:21). This provides a basic framework for differentiating between the secular (state) and the sacred (church).

2. Paul reiterates this same truth in Romans 13:7, where he uses the same word for "render" as Jesus did in Matthew 22:21. Paul writes, "Render to all what is due them: tax to whom tax is due; custom to whom custom; fear to whom fear; honor to whom honor." By pointing back to Christ's words, Paul affirms the same distinction between the secular and the sacred.

3. Peter also echoes Christ's teaching from Matthew 22:21 in 1 Peter 2:17 when he distinguishes between fearing God and honoring the king. Peter further addresses the different spheres of authority in 1 Peter 2–3. The sacred sphere of the church is addressed in 1 Peter 2:1-10. The secular sphere of society and government is addressed in 1 Peter 2:11-17; 3:8-17. A third sphere, that of the household (which in Roman times included servants), is addressed in 1 Peter 2:18-20; 3:1-7.

4. In 1 Corinthians 6:1-9, Paul applies this principle to the believers in Corinth. They were not to take their internal disputes to a secular court, but rather, were to appeal to the spiritual authority of the church for resolution. Disagreements between believers are to be resolved in the sphere of the sacred, not the sphere of the secular. Paul's exhortation is clear:

> Does any one of you, when he has a case against his neighbor, dare to go to law before the unrighteous and not before the saints? Or do you not know that the saints will judge the world? If the world is judged by you, are you not competent to constitute the smallest law courts? Do you not know that we will judge angels? How much more matters of this life? So if you have law courts dealing with matters of this life, do you appoint them as judges who are of no account in the church? I say this to your shame. Is it so, that there is not among you one wise

man who will be able to decide between his brethren, but brother goes to law with brother, and that before unbelievers? Actually, then, it is already a defeat for you, that you have lawsuits with one another. Why not rather be wronged? Why not rather be defrauded? On the contrary, you yourselves wrong and defraud. You do this even to your brethren. Or do you not know that the unrighteous will not inherit the kingdom of God?

As those who belong to the kingdom of God, we should not delegate to secular authorities that which ought to be handled within the sphere of the church.

5. In addition to the state and the church, God has also ordained the family as a societal structure designed to promote good and curtail wickedness (Exodus 20:12; Ephesians 6:1-4). These structures were designed by God to uphold the fabric of society. Without the structures of the family, the church, and the government, society would quickly spiral into anarchy and chaos.

6. We acknowledge that overlap exists between these spheres of authority. But in general, citizens are to submit to the government *in civil matters* (Romans 13:1-7), children are to submit to parents *in family matters* (Ephesians 6:1-2), and believers are to submit to their elders *in ecclesiastical matters* (1 Corinthians 16:16; Hebrews 13:7). The author of Hebrews articulates the proper response to spiritual authority with these words: "Obey your leaders and submit to them, for they keep watch over your souls as those who will give an account. Let them do this with joy and not with grief, for this would be unprofitable for you" (Hebrews 13:17).

7. Those in positions of spiritual authority in the church should not abdicate their God-given role to the government. Pastors and elders will give an account to Christ for how they have shepherded the flock entrusted to their care. Consider Peter's encouragement to his fellow elders:

I exhort the elders among you, as your fellow elder and witness of the sufferings of Christ, and a partaker also of the glory that is to be revealed, shepherd the flock of God among you, exercising oversight not under compulsion, but voluntarily, according to the will of God; and not for sordid gain, but with eagerness; nor yet as lording it over those allotted to your charge, but proving to be examples to the flock. And when the Chief Shepherd appears, you will receive the unfading crown of glory (1 Peter 5:1-4).

8. The distinctions between these spheres of authority become an issue when they are in conflict with one another. When the civil government interferes with the worship, doctrine, or polity of the church, it has overstepped its God-given jurisdiction. To borrow the words of Jesus from Matthew 22:21, Caesar is meddling in things that belong to God.

9. This principle has been understood throughout the centuries within Protestant church history. It was also part of the founding principles of religious freedom in the United States (and in other Western nations where a line of separation is drawn between church and state). The historical example of the Puritans and the Scottish Covenanters, in response to the state-mandated Book of Common Prayer, provides a compelling precedent. Those sixteenth- and seventeenth-century believers were willing to give up their careers, their freedom, and even their lives to safeguard their churches from governmental interference and encroachment.

PONDERING THESE PRINCIPLES

As we reflect on these five biblical principles, we recognize we are first and foremost followers of the Lord Jesus and citizens of His kingdom. As such, He commands us to respond to civil authorities with an attitude of submission and respect. Recognizing that God has ordained governmental authority, we seek to be obedient (in action) and submissive (in attitude) to those whom God has placed in positions of authority over us.

We simultaneously recognize that Christ has placed spiritual leaders over the church, who are accountable directly to Him for how they shepherd the flock under their care. Governing officials do not have jurisdiction over the worship, doctrine, or polity of the church. This truth is not only biblical, it is recognized by the First Amendment of the Constitution of the United States. When government oversteps its God-ordained sphere of authority and places unbiblical restrictions on the church, believers will not be able to comply. As a result, Christians may face persecution and suffering for their unwillingness to fall in line.

Because secular governments are often at odds with the church, Christians can expect to be persecuted by those in positions of governmental authority. When that occurs, we must not respond with vitriol, vengeance, or violence. Instead, we demonstrate an attitude of submission by suffering honorably. Our desire should be to live as law-abiding citizens not only to avoid the ire of the government, but more importantly, because we seek (a) to obey the law of God, and (b) to exhibit a compelling testimony of righteousness and love to the unbelieving world around us.

In the next chapter, we will consider what the Bible teaches about civil disobedience. We will also discuss how our elders applied these principles in response to the health restrictions and government lockdowns we faced.

CHAPTER 12

BIBLICAL EXCEPTIONS AND PASTORAL IMPLICATIONS

Nathan Busenitz

I n the previous chapter, we saw that the Bible calls believers to submit to governing authorities. This is because God has ordained governing authorities and appointed those in government to their various roles and responsibilities. Christians are expected to be law-abiding citizens who observe the ordinances and laws issued by governing officials.

However, there are exceptions to this rule. As we have already seen, the Lord Jesus did not always comply with the regulations and restrictions imposed by the leaders of Israel. When we consider the whole counsel of Scripture, we find other such examples. These exceptions pertain to times when it is appropriate or even necessary for believers to disobey the government.

In this chapter, we will consider five categories of exceptions before looking at five areas of practical implication. The previous chapter was arranged using numbered subpoints to expand and clarify each point. We will follow that same format here.

EXCEPTION 1:
AN ORDER TO DO WHAT IS WRONG

When a governing authority issues a command or a decree that requires citizens to violate God's law, believers are duty-bound to obey God and disobey the government. Put simply, if those in positions of civil authority order people to sin, believers must not comply with that order.

1. This is the most clear-cut exception in Scripture. When a government requires believers to disobey God, we must obey God rather than men. Numerous biblical examples demonstrate this principle. Consider the following:

- The wife of Joseph's master ordered Joseph to commit fornication. Joseph rightly refused, because to comply would have been to sin against God (Genesis 39:7-10).

- Pharaoh ordered the Hebrew midwives to kill every Israelite baby boy. But the midwives feared God more than Pharaoh, so they refused to comply (Exodus 1:17-21).

- The king of Jericho ordered Rahab to give up the two Israelite spies who had come to her house. Rahab feared the Lord more than the king, so she refused to reveal where the spies were hiding (Joshua 2:2-7).

- When Saul commanded his servants to kill the priests of the Lord, they refused to do so (1 Samuel 22:17).

- Shadrach, Meshach, and Abednego were commanded to bow down before a graven image, in violation of the second commandment (Exodus 20:4-5). They refused and were thrown into a fiery furnace (Daniel 3:8-23).

- Herod ordered the magi to report to him the location of baby Jesus. Instead, after being warned by God in a dream, they returned home by a different way (Matthew 2:8-12).

- The Antichrist and false prophet will order people living during the tribulation period to take the mark of the beast. This mark will be required to buy food or engage in commerce. True believers will refuse to do so (Revelation 13:15-17).

2. It is important at this point, to note the role of the conscience in such matters. The Bible teaches it is wrong to violate one's conscience (Romans 14:22-23) because the conscience reflects the law of God in the heart (Romans 2:15). On the one hand, we obey the government to maintain a clear conscience (Romans 13:5). On the other hand, believers should not follow a government mandate that causes them to violate their conscience.

3. Regarding matters of conscience, believers should be careful not to cause other Christians to stumble (1 Corinthians 8:9). They also should refrain from passing judgment on other Christians when those believers respond differently to a conscience issue (Romans 14:1-4).

4. Believers should be respectful to authorities when they cannot comply, but they should be resolute in their obedience to God's commands (Daniel 1:8-13; 1 Peter 3:15). They can maintain an attitude of submission even when engaging in an action of noncompliance.

5. The early Christian martyrs serve as a powerful example from church history. Polycarp, for instance, defied the Roman governor when told to renounce Christ. In response, Polycarp famously said, "Eighty and six years have I served Him, and He never did me any injury. How then could I blaspheme my Savior and my King?"

EXCEPTION 2:
AN ORDER TO STOP DOING
WHAT IS RIGHT

This category represents the converse of the exception outlined above. If governing officials command believers to stop doing what

God commands them to do, they must continue in obedience to God. To fail to do what the Lord commands constitutes disobedience to Him.

1. The following biblical examples illustrate this principle. They present a positive picture of those who disobeyed an earthly authority in order to comply with the commands of God.

- Pharaoh attempted to stop Moses from leading the Israelites out of Egypt. Moses disobeyed Pharaoh to obey God's directive (Exodus 5–11).

- Daniel was commanded to stop praying for a month. But he refused to stop and was thrown into a den of lions (Daniel 6:6-13).

- Persian law prohibited anyone from approaching the king without his invitation. Esther violated that law in order to save her people (Esther 4:16).

- Peter and the apostles were ordered to stop preaching about Jesus, but they refused to comply (Acts 4:19-20; 5:29-32).

2. Daniel's example is particularly powerful in this regard. The injunction not to pray was temporary. Daniel could have complied, knowing the law would be over in thirty days. He could have prayed silently. Instead, "when Daniel knew that the document was signed, he entered his house (now in his roof chamber he had windows open toward Jerusalem); and he continued kneeling on his knees three times a day, praying and giving thanks before his God, as he had been doing previously" (Daniel 6:10).

3. During the pandemic, a number of biblical commands compelled our elders to disregard certain governmental restrictions. Continued obedience to these commands meant we were unable to comply with certain civil mandates. Examples include

the command not to forsake meeting together regularly (Hebrews 10:24-25); the command to sing to the Lord in congregational worship (Ephesians 5:19-21; Colossians 3:16-17); and the command to fellowship with one another in ways that require physical closeness (Acts 6:6; Galatians 2:9; cf. Romans 16:16; 1 Corinthians 16:20; 2 Corinthians 13:12; 1 Thessalonians 5:26).

4. Historical examples of this principle would include the church of the catacombs, whose members refused to stop meeting; William Tyndale, who refused to stop translating the Bible; John Bunyan, who refused to stop preaching; and missionaries in closed countries who refuse to stop evangelizing. In such cases, faithfulness to Christ came at great personal cost, in the form of persecution and suffering.

EXCEPTION 3:
AN ORDER THAT CONTRADICTS
ANOTHER LEVEL OF CIVIL AUTHORITY

Believers often find themselves under multiple layers or levels of governing authority. In such situations, they can appeal to or seek protection from the governing authority that is most sympathetic to their cause. For example, if a lower governing authority contradicts a higher governing authority, believers can appeal to the higher authority to avoid obeying the order issued by the lower authority.

1. In the Old Testament, we find an example of this principle in the life of Queen Esther, who appealed to the king (a higher authority) in order to overcome the malicious intentions of a lesser authority, Haman (Esther 7:1-6). Centuries earlier, Hushai the Archite pretended to serve Absalom (an illegitimate authority) in order to obey the rightful ruler, King David (2 Samuel 15:32-37; 16:16-18; 17:5-20).

2. In the New Testament, examples of this principle primarily come from the life of the apostle Paul. When asked by the local magistrates to leave Philippi, Paul refused and appealed instead to his rights as a Roman citizen. Acts 16:37-40 tells the story:

Paul said to them, "They have beaten us in public without trial, men who are Romans, and have thrown us into prison; and now are they sending us away secretly? No indeed! But let them come themselves and bring us out." The policemen reported these words to the chief magistrates. They were afraid when they heard that they were Romans, and they came and appealed to them, and when they had brought them out, they kept begging them to leave the city. They went out of the prison and entered the house of Lydia, and when they saw the brethren, they encouraged them and departed.

On another occasion, Paul avoided being flogged by a Roman centurion by appealing to his rights as a Roman citizen (Acts 22:25-29). He later appealed to the Roman governor (Felix) when he was falsely accused by some religious leaders (Acts 24). Finally, Paul appealed to Caesar rather than allowing a lesser authority to determine his fate (Acts 25:11).

3. This principle demonstrates that it is appropriate for believers to work within the context of legislative or legal authority to override or undo a governing mandate. In the United States, for example, the judicial system serves as an appropriate check and balance to executive and legislative powers. The American founding fathers designed a system of checks and balances to provide citizens with these kinds of protections.

4. Historically, the Reformers found protection from persecuting popes and emperors by appealing to local magistrates, including princes and city councils. Martin Luther was protected by Prince Frederick III of Saxony. Ulrich Zwingli was protected by the Zurich city council. John Calvin, similarly, was protected by the Geneva city council. In these ways, the Reformers simultaneously submitted to one level of governing authority while finding themselves at odds with another level of governing authority.

EXCEPTION 4:
AN ORDER TO STAY SILENT
IN THE FACE OF EVIL

If a governing authority openly violates the law of God, believers are right to condemn the wickedness of that authority. While we are called to have an attitude of submission to those in authority over us, it is not wrong to rebuke their sinful behavior. Calling our leaders to righteousness is not inconsistent with an attitude of submission.

1. The Bible is replete with examples of bold figures who courageously confronted corrupt and wicked rulers:

- The prophet Nathan confronted David regarding his adultery with Bathsheba (2 Samuel 12:1-15).

- Elijah confronted Ahab for leading Israel into idolatry (1 Kings 18:17-18). He later confronted him regarding Naboth's vineyard (1 Kings 21).

- The prophet Jeremiah was incarcerated, and even left to die in a well, because he refused to give a good report about what would happen in Jerusalem (Jeremiah 38).

- John the Baptist publicly rebuked Herod for his incest and adultery (Matthew 14:1-12).

- The author of Hebrews commends the prophets, including those who were tortured and imprisoned, for their faith (Hebrews 11:32-38). They are commended for their boldness in confronting the wickedness of their day.

2. When believers condemn wickedness, they should do so in a way that maintains an attitude of respect toward those in authority. Paul's example in Acts 23:2-5 is instructive in this regard. There, we read,

The high priest Ananias commanded those standing beside him to strike him on the mouth. Then Paul said to him, "God is going to strike you, you whitewashed wall! Do you sit to try me according to the Law, and in violation of the Law order me to be struck?" But the bystanders said, "Do you revile God's high priest?" And Paul said, "I was not aware, brethren, that he was high priest; for it is written, You shall not speak evil of a ruler of your people."

3. As followers of the Lord Jesus, we do not seek to be trouble-makers or rabble-rousers (1 Timothy 2:2). But we are called to live as a light in a dark world (Ephesians 5:6-10). Collectively, the church operates as a restraining influence on society (cf. Proverbs 4:18-19; Matthew 5:12-15). It is right for both our words and our actions to serve as a rebuke to the wickedness of the culture around us. In this way, we shine as a beacon for the gospel (cf. Matthew 5:16).

EXCEPTION 5:
AN ORDER TO TURN YOURSELF IN

When a governing authority is persecuting the people of God, believers are permitted to flee and hide. They are not to respond with violence, but they are also not required to turn themselves in to a wicked authority that seeks their destruction.

1. Throughout Scripture, it is not uncommon for God's people to flee persecution or to go into hiding. The following examples illustrate that point:

- Jonathan ignored his father's order to kill David, and instead, helped David hide (1 Samuel 19:1-2; 20).

- David fled from Saul when Saul tried to kill him (1 Samuel 19:11-12, 18; 21:10).

- Obadiah hid the prophets of God from Jezebel (1 Kings 18:3-4).

- Judean officials encouraged Jeremiah and Baruch to hide from the wrath of King Jehoiakim (Jeremiah 36:19).

- Joseph and Mary fled from Herod to protect the life of baby Jesus (Matthew 2:13-15).

- Saul (Paul) fled from Damascus to avoid capture (Acts 9:23-24).

2. When believers disobey the government, in order to obey God, they should be willing to accept the consequences without violence. The Bible allows believers to flee and hide, but when found, they are not to resist or respond with anger or revenge (Acts 5:40-42).

EXERCISING THE EXCEPTIONS

As these biblical exceptions indicate, even in the sphere of civil matters, the Bible designates times when believers are not required to obey civil authority. When governing officials order believers to sin (either by committing a transgression or by ceasing to obey God's law), believers must disobey the government. In addition, if a lower magistrate issues a mandate that is contrary to a higher civil authority, believers have the right to appeal to that higher authority to effect a desired change.

When rulers act wickedly, believers are right to condemn that behavior. Christians are not being insubordinate when they call their leaders to live according to God's law. Also, when the state persecutes Christians for their faith, believers have the freedom to flee that persecution. They are not sinning when they go into hiding or meet in secret. However, when arrested, they ought to suffer for the sake of Christ with an attitude of submission.

When we interpret scriptural commands about being obedient and submissive to the government, we should do so in a way that allows for these biblical exceptions. The categories outlined above inform our understanding of Romans 13, 1 Peter 2, and similar passages.

PRACTICAL IMPLICATIONS

Given the unprecedented nature of the global pandemic and how governments responded to it, Christians found themselves asking questions they had not needed to ask before. In this section, we will present five practical questions, along with the way our churches sought to answer those questions. These answers reflect the practical implications of the principles and exceptions outlined above.

Question 1: How should we practice the relevant biblical principles?

As we consider the five biblical principles outlined in the previous chapter, we might ask ourselves how those principles ought to be applied today. In particular, how did our elders implement these principles to the situation surrounding the pandemic? The points below seek to demonstrate how each principle was put into practice.

1. *The Principle of Supreme Allegiance:* As those who affirm the supremacy of Christ, we look to His Word as our final authority for how to navigate these issues (cf. 2 Timothy 3:16-17). We direct our people to do the same as we work to strengthen their resolve by buttressing them with the truths of Scripture.

2. *The Principle of Sovereign Appointment:* Knowing God is sovereign over all human kingdoms and governments allows us to trust Him even when those in authority act contrary to His law. It gives us confidence when we pray with the knowledge that He reigns over all the earth—including modern nations and governments.

3. *The Principle of Secular Animosity:* We understand that those who love the Lord will be hated by the world. Consequently, we

should be prepared to face hostility from unbelievers, including those in positions of political power. We should not be surprised when we are called to suffer for the sake of Christ.

4. *The Principle of a Submissive Attitude:* To whatever degree possible, given these principles and exceptions, believers seek to live in subjection to governing authorities. This subjection is seen in actions of obedience and attitudes of submission. Even when compliance is not possible, we should still be characterized by humility, kindness, respect, and grace.

5. *The Principle of Spheres of Authority:* When civil authorities meddle in matters of worship, doctrine, or church polity, the pastors and elders of each local congregation are to exercise their God-given prerogative to shepherd the flock (1 Peter 5:1-4). They should not abdicate their God-given responsibilities by delegating such matters to the civil government.

Question 2: How should we exercise the biblical exceptions?

Believers are to maintain an attitude of submission toward those in authority. But there will be times when Christians cannot comply with a specific government order or mandate. As noted above, the Bible identifies several categories of exceptions. When believers ignore these categories, they can get themselves in trouble. An extreme but useful example of this is German churches at the outset of World War II that supported the Nazi party on the basis of Romans 13. Faithful Christians understand the biblical exceptions and act accordingly.

1. *Not Doing What Is Wrong:* When a government requires its citizens to do something that is contrary to the law of God, believers are duty-bound not to comply. This includes instances in which a government mandate would cause a Christian to violate his or her conscience. For example, when people at Grace Community Church asked our pastors whether they should get the vaccine, we encouraged them to follow their conscience and trust the Lord. This

counsel was in keeping with the principles found in 1 Corinthians 8–10 and Romans 14–15.

2. *Continuing to Do What Is Right:* When civil authorities order us to stop doing that which the Bible commands, we cannot comply with those prohibitions. As noted above, believers are commanded not to forsake meeting together regularly (Hebrews 10:24-25). Christians are also commanded to sing in worship (Ephesians 5:19-21; Colossians 3:16-17). We are further commanded to fellowship in ways that require physical closeness (Acts 6:6; Galatians 2:9; cf. Romans 16:16; 1 Corinthians 16:20; 2 Corinthians 13:12; 1 Thessalonians 5:26). When government health mandates prohibited those actions, we felt we had no choice but to disregard those prohibitions.

3. *Appealing to a Higher Authority:* Christians in the United States have the right to appeal to higher legal authorities (e.g., the US Supreme Court and the Constitution). This is precisely what the leadership of Grace Community Church did when they filed a lawsuit against Los Angeles county and the state of California. The purpose of that legal action was to get protection and relief for our church in the face of interference from local and state government officials.

4. *Confronting Corruption:* When civil authorities exercise their authority in an unbiblical way, it is right for believers to call them to repent. Pastor MacArthur modeled this when he repeatedly called out the ways politicians were manipulating the pandemic for their own political ends.

5. *Freedom to Flee or Hide:* When civil authorities attempt to prevent the church from meeting, it is appropriate for believers to meet secretly. But it would not be right for believers to respond with retribution or violence of any kind (John 18:36). For example, when GraceLife Church was fenced off by Albertan authorities, the church members did not physically resist the government's efforts. However, the church began meeting in undisclosed locations to avoid governmental interference with their Sunday services.

6. *Willingness to Suffer:* Our elders were willing to accept the consequences for our actions, doing so in a peaceable manner toward those in positions of civil authority. We did not incite violent protests or angry tirades. We simply continued to meet as we had always done.

Question 3: In situations like this, how can we faithfully pastor our people?

The circumstances surrounding COVID-19 raised unprecedented shepherding challenges, especially for churches in the Western world, where Christians have long enjoyed freedom of religion. In navigating the issues related to COVID-19, our elders recognized three important realities. They are outlined below.

1. First, we knew not every church would approach this issue the same way we did. We respected the fact that the spiritual leaders of each local church had the God-given responsibility to shepherd their flock as they believed was right before the Lord (1 Peter 5:1-4). We recognize that situations like these involve a great deal of thought and wisdom in the application of biblical principles. Consequently, different churches might apply these principles differently while still honoring the Lord (Romans 14:10-12). Our primary concern was that pastors and elders not abdicate their biblical responsibility to shepherd the flock. Spiritual leaders should always exhibit courage. That said, courageous leadership can look different in different contexts.

2. Second, we recognized not everyone in our congregation would view this issue in precisely the same way we did. We sought to be sensitive in matters of conscience while informing the minds of our people with truth. Believers might apply these principles differently within their given context. They should not violate their conscience (Romans 14:22-23), nor should they cause another believer to violate his conscience (Romans 14:13).

3. Third, we also understood some of our members might truly

be at risk, due either to age or to an underlying health condition. For that reason, we continued to provide alternative ways for people to watch the Sunday service. This was done by providing outside overflow seating and livestreaming.

4. Finally, we exercised patience with those who took longer to be convinced (1 Thessalonians 5:13). This flowed from our recognition that these individuals' consciences needed to be informed and strengthened.

Our elders regularly met with and encouraged congregants who were struggling with how to respond to the pandemic. In this regard, we sought to exercise 2 Timothy 2:25 with those who disagreed with our position on the issue.

Question 4: What is the best way to demonstrate love for the lost?

During the lockdown, we were sometimes accused of being a bad testimony to the watching world. We were told that we were not loving our neighbors because we were gathering each Sunday for church. How did we respond to those allegations, knowing the importance of loving the lost in order to be a light to the world?

1. We understand that our behavior as believers either adorns the gospel or detracts from it. This is why we seek to be submissive to governing authorities as it relates to civil matters (Titus 3:1-2). This was Peter's point when he instructed his readers to submit to those in authority in 1 Peter 2:13-17, as evidenced by his exhortation earlier in verses 11-12: "Beloved, I urge you as aliens and strangers to abstain from fleshly lusts which wage war against the soul. Keep your behavior excellent among the Gentiles, so that in the thing in which they slander you as evildoers, they may because of your good deeds, as they observe them, glorify God in the day of visitation."

2. As noted earlier, our allegiance is first and foremost to Christ. Hence, when believers are obedient to Christ's commands, they provide a powerful witness to the watching world. That witness is especially bright when their behavior runs contrary to the culture

(cf. 1 Peter 3:15-17). The light of the gospel shines brightest when the world becomes the darkest (Matthew 5:14-16).

3. Consequently, we believe it is right to prioritize love for God (the greatest commandment) over love for others (the second greatest commandment). Insofar as a perceived conflict exists between those two priorities, our love for God must have first place. To state this commitment another way: Our efforts to fulfill the second greatest commandment must never be at the expense of our duty to the greatest commandment.

4. Our love for the Lord is evidenced in our obedience to Him (John 14:15; 15:14). Our church leadership's commitment to the greatest commandment motivated our desire to obey the Lord by continuing to meet regularly (Hebrews 10:24-25).

5. In this situation, we were further convinced the best way our church could continue to be a beacon of truth and a light to the world around us was by continuing to meet. To stop meeting would not only remove our witness, it is contrary to the biblical standard (Matthew 5:14-16). We did not want to be like salt that loses its influence by being absent (Luke 14:34-35).

6. The greatest need of lost people is spiritual, not physical. Hence, the church ought to prioritize the spiritual well-being of others over their physical health. When churches across North America shut down for the sake of physical health, the result took a serious spiritual toll on society.

7. As those called to be a witness, we are also commanded to pray for governing authorities. This prayer includes an evangelistic focus (1 Timothy 2:1-7). We desire to see the lost come to saving faith, including those in positions of political power.

8. Being a light in this world includes being a beacon of the truth. As truth-bearers, it would be wrong for us to perpetuate widespread deception or to cooperate knowingly with a politicized misinformation campaign (cf. 1 Corinthians 13:6; Ephesians 5:11). While we were eager to care for the sick, we had no desire to participate

in or support the obvious politicization of COVID-19 (cf. Proverbs 21:12).

Question 5: How can we get ready for the future?

The pandemic served as a reminder for Christians to stand firm, knowing that society and the government are both growing increasingly hostile to a biblical worldview. These events provided a critical test case. The next round may involve Critical Race Theory, the LGBTQ movement, or some other social issue. Whatever the catalyst, the church must be ready to stand with courage and boldness for Christ.

1. Believers in North America needed a wake-up call. The COVID-19 pandemic served to sound that alarm. The question is how well the church responded to that test. In 2020, politicians were able to shut down churches with minimal pushback. The church was sifted, and the negligence and timidity of some was exposed (cf. 1 Peter 4:17). Whether or not the church will have the backbone to stand up to government overreach in the future remains to be seen.

2. Individually and corporately, Christians must exhibit the courage necessary to obey Christ no matter the cost. The command to be courageous reverberates throughout Scripture (Psalm 21:34; 1 Corinthians 16:13; 2 Timothy 1:7). The heroes of the faith were those who put their trust in God into bold action (cf. Hebrews 11). This courage is rooted in convictions about the lordship of Christ and the call to be loyal to Him. We take heart in His words to His disciples, "All authority has been given to Me in heaven and on earth…and lo, I am with you always, even to the end of the age" (Matthew 28:18-20; cf. Hebrews 13:5-6).

3. As those who desire to glorify God in all things (1 Corinthians 10:31), we seek to live in ways that are pleasing to Christ (2 Corinthians 5:9; Colossians 1:10). To that end, we commit ourselves to Him and His care, even when we are unable to comply with governmental regulations or restrictions. To God be the glory.

CHAPTER 13

THE TIME HAS COME

James Coates

*The next three chapters are adapted from sermons preached
in relation to the pandemic, and have been edited for use
in this book. These chapters express the biblical principles
that undergirded the stand we sought to take. The message
adapted in this chapter was delivered on December 20, 2020.*

We are going to organize our thoughts around a series of questions and answers: What is the church? Who is the head of the church? What is the gathering? What elements are essential for the corporate gathering? Why do we gather? Are we permitted to gather at present? Does the government have the authority to prevent us from gathering? Let's consider these questions one by one.

WHAT IS THE CHURCH?

To answer this, we need to address it on two levels: *universal* and *local*. The universal church is comprised of all those who have new life in Christ. The church is also in heaven, but for the sake of this discussion, let's limit our scope to all believers in the world today.

They are the redeemed, the called, the justified, the new covenant people of God, the bride of Christ, and the body of Christ.

The local or visible church is a group of believers who come together in a local assembly to accomplish specific, divinely ordained purposes clearly outlined in the New Testament. These purposes include worship, edification, participation in the ordinances, and evangelism. Because the church is the means by which God is displaying His manifold wisdom and glory in the world today to the rulers and authorities in the heavenly places (Ephesians 3:10), it is critically important that the church be visible and gather into local assemblies. It ought to order itself in accordance with the New Testament with elders and deacons and function as a place where the Word of God is preached, the gospel is proclaimed, the ordinances are practiced, the one-anothers are put into action, and believers are being built up to spiritual maturity.

There is no way to be a faithful Christian without being vitally connected to a local church. Many of the imperatives of the New Testament require belonging to a local body of believers. It is impossible to be obedient to Christ and not be active in the local church.

So, what is the church? The church is the universal body of believers that gathers into local assemblies to accomplish the Great Commission (Matthew 28:18-20).

WHO IS THE HEAD OF THE CHURCH?

We could rephrase this question, Who is the head of the body? Is Caesar the head of the body? Is a lead pastor the head of the body? Are the elders the head of the body? No, Christ alone is the head of the body. "[God] put all things in subjection under His feet, and gave Him as head over all things to the church, which is His body, the fullness of Him who fills all in all" (Ephesians 1:22-23). Jesus Christ is the head of the church. That is true of the universal church as well as each individual local church. "He is also head of the body, the church" (Colossians 1:18), referring again there to Christ.

Headship represents authority. Jesus is the supreme and ultimate authority over the church, both universal and local. That means He is the sole and final authority on all matters related to the church. He alone possesses the right to govern each local assembly. He does this through His Word as local churches organize themselves according to the teachings of Scripture. The Word of God is clear that local churches are to be organized under a plurality of biblically qualified elders who are also members of the body and have a stewardship to preach, teach, and implement the truths of God's Word. For this stewardship, the elders will be held accountable by Jesus Christ Himself.

So, who is the head of the church? Not Caesar. Not the government. Not the health authority. Jesus Christ alone is the Lord over His church.

WHAT IS THE GATHERING?

Here, we ask, What is *the* gathering? Not what is *a* gathering. For example, is a Bible study *the* gathering? Is a women's ministry *the* gathering? Is an elders' meeting *the* gathering? Is youth ministry *the* gathering? No, none of these are *the* gathering. Each of those constitutes only *a* gathering. Why? Because these smaller groups represent segments of the body. When these groups gather, most of the body is absent. They are gatherings but they aren't *the* gathering.

What is necessary for *the* gathering? The full body of Christ with its elders and deacons must come together for corporate worship. The first day of the week, both biblically and historically, has been set apart for this purpose. This is because Jesus rose from the grave on a Sunday, and the church was birthed into existence on a Sunday on the Day of Pentecost (Acts 2). The corporate gathering takes place when the entire family is present, coming together to worship God and minister to one another. The gathering is a foretaste of heaven, when all the redeemed will be together in the presence of Christ.

WHAT ELEMENTS ARE ESSENTIAL
FOR THE CORPORATE GATHERING?

This question focuses on those elements that the head of the church, the Lord Jesus Christ, stipulated as essential in His Word. These include the following:

First, the public proclamation of the Word of God is an essential component of the public gathering. In 2 Timothy 4:2, Paul told Timothy to "preach the word; be ready in season and out of season; reprove, rebuke, exhort with great patience and instruction." Here, the word "preach" calls for a public proclamation of Scripture by a man of God (2 Timothy 3:16-17).

The second essential element is the public reading of Scripture. Paul wrote, "Until I come, give attention to the public reading of Scripture, to exhortation and teaching" (1 Timothy 4:13). The corporate gathering should include a regular and extended reading of Scripture.

Often connected with that is, third, corporate prayer. We are called to "pray without ceasing" (1 Thessalonians 5:17). We are called to "pray at all times in the Spirit" (Ephesians 6:18). How much more should we do this corporately! In Romans 15:5-6, Paul gave the church in Rome the following instruction: "May the God who gives perseverance and encouragement grant you to be of the same mind with one another according to Christ Jesus, so that with one accord you may with one voice [literally, 'one mouth'] glorify the God and Father of our Lord Jesus Christ." The unified voice of the congregation implies corporate prayer. Elsewhere, Paul exhorted those in the church to pray for governing authorities (1 Timothy 2:1-7).

The fourth element is corporate singing. Ephesians 5:18-19 says, "Do not get drunk with wine, for that is dissipation"—and here's the command—"but be filled with the Spirit, speaking to one another in psalms and hymns and spiritual songs, singing and making melody with your heart to the Lord." The evidence that one is filled with the Spirit is expressed in congregational worship through song.

Singing praise to the Lord is an essential component of the corporate gathering.

When the government says we cannot sing, they are forbidding what God commands and quenching the evidence of the Spirit's work in our congregation. They are opposing the Word of God. By the way, "making melody with your heart" does not mean making melody without a sound. The "your" in "your heart" is plural, while the word "heart" is singular. So a congregation is being addressed—plural—to sing with one corporate heart. Believers are to sing aloud with their mouths as part of a congregation that is of one heart and mind in worship to Christ.

A fifth essential element is fellowship. Hebrews 10:24 25 is clear in this regard: We are called to consider carefully and thoughtfully how we might provoke one another to love and good deeds, "not forsaking our own assembling together as is the habit of some, but encouraging one another; and all the more as you see the day drawing near." The author of Hebrews places the command to consider ways to encourage one another to love and good deeds with the command not to forsake the gathering of the saints. Why? Because it is necessary to come together physically to accomplish the purpose expressed in Hebrews 10:24-25.

The fellowship that takes place before, during, and after the corporate gathering is essential to the gathering. It is the one element that most obviously cannot be fulfilled virtually. A livestreamed service cuts a person off from both giving and receiving the one-anothers, and there are about sixty one-another commands in Scripture. Currently, our government is forbidding what God commands. Pastors need to understand this. The one-another commands comprise a requirement and an obligation to obey Jesus Christ. We must be together physically to accomplish this biblical mandate. What they call socializing, we call fellowship; by forbidding socializing, the government has forbidden biblical fellowship. As a result, the church must disobey the government and instead, obey God.

Sixth, the ordinances of baptism and the Lord's Supper are essential. The current situation raises an important question: Can believers turn the ordinances of the corporate gathering into something virtual without fundamentally altering what they are? Technology, though wonderful, cannot substitute for the corporate gathering of the body. If water baptism symbolizes the believer's entrance into the body of Christ, and if the Lord's table celebrates the believer's ongoing communion with Christ as part of His body, can we legitimately participate in those ordinances in isolation while staring at a screen? The Lord Jesus designed these ordinances to be observed by the corporate body. They are essential to the gathering.

The seventh essential element is church discipline. This process, articulated by Christ in Matthew 18, begins when one believer goes to another and shows them their sin. This is an aspect of fellowship. Though the first two steps of church discipline occur in private settings, the latter stages of church discipline take place corporately. This does not mean that church discipline is exercised every time the church assembles. But when the third and fourth steps of church discipline are employed, they take place corporately. To tell the assembly about a discipline situation, or to put someone out of the assembly, implies that the assembly is gathered. Thus, without the corporate gathering, it is not possible to practice church discipline in a biblical way.

In summary, then, we have highlighted seven essential elements that underscore the vital importance of the corporate gathering: the public preaching of God's Word, the public reading of Scripture, corporate prayer, corporate singing, fellowship, the ordinances, and church discipline.

WHY DO WE GATHER?

The first reason we gather is to worship: to commemorate what God has done through His Son in the gospel, and to ascribe to Him honor and glory. But we also gather for the equipping of the saints. Ephesians 4:11 says this: "He [Christ] gave some as apostles, and some as prophets, and some as evangelists, and some as pastors and teachers, for the equipping of the saints"—for what?—"for the work of service"—to what?—"to the building up of the body of Christ"— for how long?—"until we all attain to the unity of the faith, and of the knowledge of the Son of God, to a mature man, to the measure of the stature which belongs to the fullness of Christ." Our job, as a leadership team, is to equip our congregation for the work of service, so that they, in turn, do the work of service. This contributes to the maturing of the body of Christ.

In essence, the government is forbidding our people from the work of service. We cannot come together physically for Bible studies. We cannot come together physically for men's ministry, women's ministry, or youth ministry. There are no fellowship events to organize for those with the gifts of helps or hospitality. The government is forbidding us from the work of service. When we gather, we're equipping the saints for the work of service to the building up of the body of Christ. And the government is saying, "No, you can't do that work of service."

We gather to worship, and we gather to equip the saints for the work of service. But the government has forbidden the ongoing execution of that work. That places the governing authorities in opposition to God and puts us in a position where we must obey God rather than men.

The church is the universal body of believers that gathers in local assemblies to accomplish the Great Commission. Christ is the head and supreme authority of each local assembly. The gathering is when the full body of Christ, with its elders and deacons, comes together for corporate worship. The essential elements of the corporate gathering are the preaching of God's Word, the reading of Scripture, corporate prayer, singing, fellowship expressed in the one-anothers, corporate participation in the ordinances, and the practice of church discipline. And we gather for the purpose of worship and to equip the saints for the work of service, a work that is critical to the continued maturity of the body of Christ.

ARE WE PERMITTED TO GATHER?

Are we permitted, by our government, to gather at present? The obvious answer is no. We are not permitted to gather. That's why the police were here today. They were here along with officials from Alberta Health Services because we are not permitted to gather. You say, "But James, we are allowed to gather at fifteen percent." That is true. We are allowed to have *a* gathering. But we are not allowed to have *the* gathering. For ten months now, the government has forbidden us from corporate worship. To be compliant, we as elders must tell a significant portion of the body that they cannot come for worship. Think about that. As under-shepherds of the Lord Jesus Christ, we are being told by the government to tell the flock of Christ, "Sorry, you can't worship today. It's not safe. The government says so." That is the difficulty for us; struggling to tell people, "No, you can't worship today. No, you have to worship online." Do we have that authority? Can we tell people they are not allowed to come and worship?

You say, "But James, that's what you did when the pandemic began." You're right. But that was born out of ignorance: ignorance about the virus, ignorance about the proper response to our government in a situation like this. It was incredibly difficult. I had to wrestle with questions like, How do I shepherd people I can't even see? I was preaching sermons to a camera. After doing that I would return home, take off my suit coat, hang it up, and wonder, *What in the world are we doing?* I would spend all week preparing to minister the Word of God to God's people, yet I couldn't see or interact with them.

As elders, we are refusing to tell our people they can't come. Our responsibility as shepherds is to open our doors. We are opening our doors to worship. I told AHS this morning, "We do not know if we are going to be compliant today because we do not know how many people will come. We are leaving that decision up to our people. They are adults who are well-informed. They know the nature of the situation legally and medically. They come to church because they want to worship their Lord and engage in the corporate gathering."

Our responsibility as shepherds is to open our doors to facilitate God's people coming together in worship. We are unwilling to tell the people of this body that they cannot come, that they are not permitted to worship. We cannot force our people to come to church. But faithfulness, for us, is simply opening our doors and doing ministry as usual.

Admittedly, these are incredibly difficult times. We have supported those members of our church who have chosen to stay home and watch livestreamed services, provided they were convinced in their own mind, before the Lord, that they had made the right choice (Romans 14:5). But with the information we have, we refuse to forbid the flock from gathering corporately. It would be impossible for us to do this without a unified leadership. Our elders are together and united.

So, are we permitted to gather at present? The answer is no. But we are gathering anyway, and we are gathering in obedience to the supreme authority over the church, to which every knee will bow, both in heaven and on earth and under the earth, and every tongue will confess, that Jesus is Lord.

DOES THE GOVERNMENT HAVE THE AUTHORITY TO PREVENT US FROM GATHERING?

This question needs to be answered from two perspectives, both biblically and legally. Biblically, let's start with the reality that all authority is derived from God: "I am the LORD, and there is no other; besides Me there is no God" (Isaiah 45:5). That means every sphere of authority has received a delegated authority. It has been

delegated to them by God. He determines the limits on that authority. Government is a minister of God (Romans 13:4), and therefore
it must fulfill the purpose for which He appointed it. Everyone who
exercises authority is accountable to Him, whether it is a police officer, a health official, or a government leader. All human authorities
will be judged by the Lord Jesus Christ for how they exercised their
power and influence.

There are distinct spheres of authority: the home, the church,
and the government. There is a certain measure of overlap between
them. For example, murder committed in the home will bring the
enforcement arm of government and could also bring with it consequences in the church. A crime committed in the context of the
church will also bring the enforcement arm of government and
could have implications for the home.

But though there are overlaps, there are also clear lines of distinction. For example, the church does not get to make governmental
policy. The home doesn't either. Which brings us to this question:
Can the government dictate to the church how to worship? Absolutely not. The government receives its authority from God. He
sets the limits on that authority and provides ultimate accountability. Civil officials are not permitted to dictate to the church how to
worship.

Biblically, the government has no authority to tell the church
how to worship. But what about from a legal perspective? The beginning of the Canadian Charter of Rights and Freedoms explains that
it guarantees the rights and freedoms set out in it subject only to
such reasonable limits prescribed by law, as can be demonstrably justified in a free and democratic society. That means the government
is subject to the law of the land.

We often act as if the government is the law—that whatever the
government says goes. But there is a law that governs this land. The
government is subject to that law, and that law is fundamentally in
place to protect the citizens from tyrannical governments. In this

situation, we aren't the ones who are in disobedience to the law. The government is. They need to prove that what they are doing is necessary, that the infringement on our civil liberties is justifiable. It is our responsibility as citizens to hold them accountable. In fact, I would say a failure to do so would be a dereliction of our duty.

We have a responsibility to meet on legal grounds, and this, too, is tied to Scripture. The second greatest commandment is that we love our neighbor as ourselves. Right now, the civil liberties of our neighbors are being severely eroded. Nearly an entire generation of men gave their lives for our freedoms. Yet so many are simply handing over those hard-fought civil liberties without any word of protest. Not me. I'm sounding the alarm, and based on the second greatest commandment, I refuse to stay silent while our government takes away the civil liberties of an unsuspecting or unknowing generation of citizens.

So, does the government have the authority to prevent us from gathering? Not biblically, not legally, and not legitimately.

WHY IS THIS HAPPENING?

To answer this question, it is helpful to know a little eschatology. The apostle John wrote, "Children, it is the last hour; and just as you heard that antichrist is coming, even now many antichrists have appeared; from this we know it is the last hour" (1 John 2:18). That verse indicates that while there are many false teachers, there is yet one Antichrist who is to come. The apostle Paul calls him the man of lawlessness in 2 Thessalonians 2:3-4, "who opposes and exalts himself above every so-called God or object of worship." Revelation 13 indicates that during the reign of the Antichrist, everyone on earth will need a mark to buy and sell: "He causes all, the small and the great, and the rich and the poor, and the free men and the slaves, to be given a mark on their right hand or on their forehead, and he provides that no one will be able to buy or to sell, except the one who has the mark, either the name of the beast or the number of his name" (verses 16-17). The book of Revelation reveals that during the tribulation, there will be a one-world government with a one-world economy. People will need a mark to buy and sell. This is the direction everything is going, in keeping with God's sovereign plan.

It is not difficult for us to understand how this kind of one-world government might arise, with the push toward globalism gaining momentum in recent years. We don't know when these things will occur, but we can see the direction that society is heading. Western governments are using the pandemic to elevate their power by increasing people's dependence on government. Meanwhile, a leftist social agenda has infiltrated the media, pushing society toward uniformity and canceling those who protest its radical ideologies. This fits the direction history is moving as it races towards the end.

Does this mean the Lord's return is near? Well, it is nearer now than it has ever been. But we do not know when He will return. Only God knows when Jesus is coming back. Our job is to be faithful. We are to live in obedience while we watch and pray. The church is called to be a city on a hill so that the light of the gospel might shine forth (Matthew 5:14-16).

This is a call not to panic, but to be prepared. We do not know when, or even if, society will get back to normal. We will see what happens. But the bottom line is this: You need to be ready. Be ready to take a stand for the Lord Jesus Christ and to receive whatever consequences come. Those in the world are not going to understand what we are doing. But our aim and ambition are to please Christ and to be ready to stand for Him.

Also, for those who have not embraced the Lord Jesus in saving faith, you need to settle your accounts with God. You need to be ready to meet Him. Recognize that you have sinned and fallen short of the glory of God. You are guilty and helpless before a holy judge. If you die in your sins, you will suffer the righteous wrath of God for all of eternity. The only way of escape is to turn to Jesus Christ, who died on the cross to pay the penalty of sin for all who believe in Him. As Romans 10:9 explains, if you believe in your heart that God raised Jesus Christ from the dead and confess Him as Lord, you will be saved.

Statistically, it is unlikely that you will die from COVID.[35] But that does not mean that you will escape death altogether. The author of Hebrews says, "It is appointed for men to die once and after this comes judgment" (Hebrews 9:27). Death is inevitable. The only remedy for death is to place your hope in Christ. Only then can you say, with the apostle Paul, "'Death is swallowed up in victory. O death, where is your victory? O death, where is your sting?' The sting of death is sin, and the power of sin is the law; but thanks be to God, who gives us the victory through our Lord Jesus Christ" (1 Corinthians 15:55-57).

CHAPTER 14

DIRECTING
GOVERNMENT
TO ITS DUTY

James Coates

This chapter is adapted from a message preached on February
14, 2021—two days before I turned myself in to the police.

This particular time in history has exposed some deficiencies
in the broader evangelical church. For one, it has exposed a
deficient ecclesiology. Ecclesiology is the study of the doctrines of the church and encompasses everything from what the
church is to the essential elements of its worship. What is apparent,
at least to me, is that the church today has a very low ecclesiology
where virtual church is not only accepted as fine, it is considered a
wonderful evolution of things.

Related to that is, two, a deficient approach to Scripture—that
unless Scripture explicitly states certain things, there is total freedom over how we fulfill its commands. So, unless Scripture states,
"The entire congregation shall meet on Sunday, in person, ensuring
that all interaction takes place within six feet of other people, without a mask, and with some kind of physical expression of affection, whether it be a hug or handshake," we're off the hook. Such

statements typically start out like this: "Scripture doesn't explicitly say…" Those who take this stance conclude that the government isn't commanding us to sin, and therefore, we must comply. That sentiment reveals a deficient approach to Scripture and the principles it contains: that unless the Bible explicitly says something, I'm under no obligation to do it.

Why is that deficient? Because it fails to recognize that the God-intended implications of a passage are binding. As students of Scripture, we are under obligation to heed its implications, and that requires a much more careful and thoughtful approach to Scripture. The idea held by some is that it is too much to ask that Scripture speak to our current situation. Yet it certainly does speak to our current situation. But given the unique setting we find ourselves in, much of what we're dealing with is addressed by way of implication, and that requires an intensely careful and thoughtful reading of Scripture.

Third, I believe our circumstances have exposed a deficient theology of persecution. We seem to have an incredibly narrow and historically ignorant view of what persecution actually is. We seem to think persecution is only persecution when it is directed exclusively at the church, and that unless the church is being singled out, it must obey the government. Now, developing a robust theology of persecution is beyond the scope of this sermon, but we need to understand that persecution often results from doing what the state forbids, and that obedience to Christ is the catalyst for persecution. You don't wait to be persecuted to obey Christ; it is your obedience to Christ that results in persecution. Some people give the impression that if we were being persecuted, only then would it be right to gather, which is a rather strange perspective—especially because all you need to do to avoid persecution is obey the government or comply with it. If you comply with the government, then you will not be persecuted.

Further, if you say that *only* if we are being persecuted should we gather—as we currently are—then you are saying that it is right to gather. Implicitly, you are saying it is right to gather—that, according to the Word of God, if the church were being persecuted, then we would have an obligation to gather. That is an admission that it is right to gather.

Whether or not we are being persecuted makes no difference. That is not the basis upon which we ought to do anything. Our actions must be in obedience to Christ. I am quite content to let the Lord Jesus Christ Himself decide whether or not this is persecution. He promises that those who are persecuted for His name's sake will be blessed. He is the One who blesses, and I am content to leave that in His court. My responsibility is to obey Him.

Connected to this, I believe, is a deficient knowledge of history, both church and secular. We are often not very good historians. As a result, we tend to be susceptible to deception, both theological and political. We need to become better historians to protect ourselves.

Many Christians have a deficient understanding of persecution and history. But the primary deficiency I want to address in this message relates to the role of government. The current situation has revealed that many Christians have both a deficient and inaccurate theology of government. It is deficient for at least two reasons: One, we've simply had it so good for so long, and therefore have not had to think deeply about this aspect of theology. It's a muscle we simply have not exercised. Two, as noted above, we are ignorant of historical theology. Theologians of the past thought deeply about these things, and we have not sufficiently exposed ourselves to their writings.

To address this deficiency, I want to turn to Romans 13. This time, I want to look at it from a different vantage point. Instead of focusing primarily on our response to government, I want to focus on the government's God-given duty. What is the God-ordained role of government? Can we even ask that question? There is a sense in which this sermon is addressed to the government. The government needs to be informed of its God-ordained purpose and, if we, the church, don't inform them, who will? The church is to be the pillar and support of the truth (1 Timothy 3:15). We are the priests of God, called to mediate His Word to this world. Therefore, we have the responsibility of informing the government of its God-given duty. We will certainly touch on aspects of our response to the government, but the main goal is to highlight the God-ordained role of government authorities.

Romans 13:1-7 says,

> Every person is to be in subjection to the governing authorities. For there is no authority except from God, and those which exist are established by God. Therefore whoever resists authority has opposed the ordinance of God; and they who have opposed will receive condemnation upon themselves. For rulers are not a cause of fear for good behavior, but for evil. Do you want to have no fear of authority? Do what is good and you will have praise from the same; for it is a minister of God to you for good. But if you do what is evil, be afraid; for it does not bear the sword for nothing; for it is a minister of God, an avenger who brings wrath on the one who practices evil. Therefore it is necessary to be in subjection, not only because of wrath, but also for conscience' sake. For because of this you also pay taxes, for rulers are servants of God, devoting themselves to this very thing. Render to all what is due them: tax to whom tax is due; custom to whom custom; fear to whom fear; honor to whom honor.

The goal of this message is to further develop our theology of government, to assist us in navigating our ever-changing world, and, Lord willing, to even inform the government of its God-ordained role.

THE SOURCE OF GOVERNING AUTHORITY

First, *the Source of Governmental Authority*. Verse 1: "Every person is to be in subjection to the governing authorities." What does it mean to be in subjection? It means that we are to arrange ourselves under the governing authorities, to be submissive to them. Now, does submission demand obedience? Typically, yes. But it is important to note that Paul does not write, "Every person must be *absolutely obedient* to the governing authorities." There is certainly overlap between submissiveness and obedience, but obedience clearly demands more. There are times when we simply cannot obey the government. For example, Shadrach, Meshach, and Abednego, refused to bow the knee to the golden image (Daniel 3). Similarly, the apostles declared, "We must obey God rather than men" (Acts 5:29).

Is it possible, then, to be simultaneously submissive and disobedient to the government? Yes, we can practice civil disobedience while maintaining a submissive posture. How? By humbly subjecting ourselves to the consequences of our civil disobedience. We recognize we are not the government, but we have a responsibility to Christ. When that responsibility leads us into conflict with the government, we have to bear up under that conflict graciously, humbly, and submissively. The government has the right before God to do whatever they believe is right, and they will be held accountable for that. When they act unjustly, God will settle the score at the end of the day. But we can practice civil disobedience while maintaining a submissive posture. How do we do that? By entrusting ourselves to Him who judges righteously (1 Peter 2:23; 2:20). Practicing civil disobedience in one area does not mean practicing civil disobedience in every area. It is only at a specific point that civil disobedience would need to be practiced.

How do we determine when civil disobedience is necessary? Let me give you three categories: One, when the government forbids what God commands; for example, forbidding the preaching of His

Word. We cannot comply with that. Two, when the government commands what God forbids; for example, commanding worship of a golden image. We can't comply with that. And three, when the government commands what isn't theirs to command—for example, the terms of worship. We cannot comply with that. Those are three categories that call for civil disobedience.

All of that relates more toward our response to government, and we want to focus on the God-ordained role of government. We get into that in the next part of verse 1, where the reason for being subject to the governing authorities is given: "There is no authority except from God, and those which exist are established by God." The reason we are called to be subject to the governing authorities is because all authority is from above. That means that all authority originates with God. It is delegated by Him. That means the governing authorities are accountable to God. In other words, the governing authorities have a stewardship from God for which they will be judged. They are not autonomous. They are not sovereign. They are servants of God (verse 5), and servants are always accountable to their master. What must they do to faithfully discharge their duty? They must govern by the standard by which they will be judged: the Word of God.

Now, how many governments know they are accountable to God? Do you think our government knows it is accountable to God? It's not likely, and if they do, they suppress it in unrighteousness (Romans 1:18). Whose role is it to inform them or call them to repentance? The church. We have been entrusted with the revelation that spells this out. In fact, if the church refuses to fulfill this role and function, then it is walking in negligence. Such negligence is incredibly unloving, since those in authority who rule unrighteously are storing up wrath for themselves. Unless they repent, they are only adding to their eternal judgment. By not informing the government of its God-ordained role, and not pointing out when the government is out of step with that role, we are not loving the government.

These are individuals, human beings, who are accountable to God. They need to be confronted with their sin in order to realize they need to be reconciled to God through the Son, Jesus Christ. Complying with unbiblical and unjust government mandates is neither faithful nor loving. Affirming the government has an authority it doesn't have is equally unloving. It does not demonstrate true love for those in authority, or for our neighbor, or for the church. More importantly, it does not demonstrate true love for Christ. The church, of all institutions, has the obligation to call the government to its God-ordained duty.

Now, how do we do that? This is where things become more difficult because there are many benign ways to call government to its duty: you can write your member of the legislative assembly; you can write your premier or governor; or you can write an open letter to the public. There are also more confrontational ways—for example, you can take the government to court and enter into a legal dispute.

You can also do what we are doing. By meeting, we are testifying that the government has no jurisdiction here, not with regard to our worship. By simply being open and by garnering the attention we have, we are showing the government that they have overstepped their authority regardless of where they stand on the pandemic. So by us obeying Christ in this way, the government is being forced to consider what their authority actually is, in light of God's Word.

For our church to take this stand, it is obedience to Christ that is driving this. It is theology that is driving this. Jesus is the head of the church. He is the supreme authority over the church, and He governs His church by His Word. Our responsibility is to ensure that His Word governs the church. But by doing what we are doing, we are also loving our neighbor. That, too, obeys Christ. In addition, we are loving our government because we are testifying that its interference is out-of-step with its God-given role. That, too, is obedience to Christ.

Admittedly, I have not been very politically involved in the past. I have voted and I have preached the Word, which has unavoidable political implications because the Word addresses biblical morality. But that has been the extent of it. So, what has changed? For the first time in my ministry, the government is reaching into the life of the church. That is not their domain. That is the domain of the elders here at GraceLife Church. That is the Lord Jesus Christ's domain. Attempting to dictate to us the terms of worship is not the government's jurisdiction, and we refuse to render to the government what is not theirs.

By recognizing God is the source of governmental authority, things begin to become clear. Government needs to realize it is accountable to God and that it will be judged by Him in accordance with His Word. Since we have been entrusted with His Word, we have a unique responsibility whereby we must call the government to its God-ordained duty. Doing so, while maintaining a submissive posture, is among the most loving things we can do.

THE LIMITS OF GOVERNING AUTHORITY

Second, *the Limits of Governmental Authority.* Verse 2: "Therefore whoever resists authority has opposed the ordinance of God; and they who have opposed will receive condemnation upon themselves." Everyone is to be in subjection to the governing authorities. This is because a government's authority finds its source in God, and therefore, everyone who resists this authority opposes the ordinance of God. They will therefore receive earthly condemnation from the same.

But there are some questions that need to be asked at this point. For example, is all resistance to governing authority in opposition to the ordinance of God? We would have to say no. See the apostles, and Shadrach, Meshach, and Abed-nego. How about this: Is every government law an ordinance of God? Again, we would say no. Otherwise, when governments order an evil, unjust law, God would be ordering evil. So when the government orders an unjust law, it is not an ordinance of God. God does not order unjust laws. Or, in a similar way, this question: Do all government laws come with the authority of God? Once more, we would say no. Their authority is delegated to them. Consequently, their laws must be consistent with the law of God.

Here is another question: When the government says we cannot meet as we always have, does that order come with God's authority? If you say yes, then you are pitting God against God. You are implying that God is contradicting Himself, since He commands believers not to forsake the gathering of the saints. But at that point, someone could say, "This is a pandemic, so these are extenuating circumstances." Leaving questions about the severity of the health situation aside, that kind of response reveals a deficient understanding of the limits of government.

This is going to dovetail with what we'll see next, *The Purpose of Governmental Authority.* But the limits and purpose of government authority go hand in hand. The God-ordained purpose of something places limits on it; the government has a particular lane.

To begin, let's consider Genesis 1:26-28. This passage describes the overarching kingdom mandate given to mankind. This transcends every legal document that governs a land. So, this transcends the Canadian Charter. In fact, I would say that the US Constitution, according to its founders, sought to uphold what Genesis teaches.

> God said, "Let Us make man in Our image, according to Our likeness; and let them rule over the fish of the sea and over the birds of the sky and over the cattle and over all the earth, and over every creeping thing that creeps on the earth." God created man in His own image, in the image of God He created him; male and female He created them. God blessed them; and God said to them,

"Be fruitful and multiply, and fill the earth, and subdue
it; and rule over the fish of the sea and over the birds of
the sky and over every living thing that moves on the
earth."

God gave man the unique responsibility to exercise dominion
over the earth, to rule and subdue the earth. This is an inalienable
right given by God to man. It is an undeniable right, and by right, I
mean authority. God has given humanity the authority to rule and
subdue the earth.

That comes with certain freedoms: There is the right to life.
That is, the right to live the life that God has given to you up until
He takes it away. There is the right to work. In giving to men the
responsibility to rule over the earth, work is a fundamental, inalienable right. The Bible says, "You do not work, you do not eat." Work
is a right given to men by God. There is the right to have a family,
the right to be with your family, the right to be with family when
they are dying—those are God-given, inalienable rights. Also, the
right to acquire property, to possess property, to own property is
part of ruling and subduing the earth. It is part of exercising dominion over the earth.

If man is going to rule over the earth and exercise dominion and
carry out his inalienable, God-given rights, what does he need, especially in a fallen world? He needs government. Why? Government is
in a place to protect people's inalienable rights. The purpose of government is to facilitate mankind's role in exercising dominion over
the earth. The government is fundamentally there to make sure we
can fulfill our mission: to subdue the earth, to work, to worship, to
be fruitful and multiply. The government is a God-ordained institution put in place to ensure law and order, and to protect these God-
given rights. So government is vital to mankind's ability to fulfill this
mission, especially in a fallen world.

One of the earliest times, if not the earliest time, that government is implied is in Genesis 9, in relation to murder: "Whoever

sheds man's blood, by man his blood shall be shed, for in the image of God He made man" (verse 6). As early as Genesis 9, we have a clear reference to government in connection with the death penalty. Now fundamentally, what is that protecting? Is it protecting life? Well, it certainly isn't protecting the life of the one who was murdered; he is already dead. So, what is it protecting? Inalienable rights, and in this case, the right to life. What effect is the death penalty supposed to have? It is designed to prevent murder, which, in turn, protects a person's God-given right to live—at least until God takes that person's life away.

The right to life is only one of those God-given freedoms. The government's responsibility is to protect those *rights*, of which life is but one. It is a package deal. The government is responsible to uphold all the inalienable rights given to men by God. Those in power must be careful not to prioritize one right to such an extent that they trample on others. Therein lies the entire problem at present.

This is critical to understanding the limits and purpose of government: Man is made in God's image; God has given to man the authority to exercise dominion over the earth; and this invests him with certain inalienable rights to accomplish that end. To facilitate this, God put government in place, and its responsibility is to protect these inalienable rights so that man can accomplish his mission. In this way, the government is "a minister of God to [us] for good."

If the government does its job to ensure that your God-given rights are protected, are you not going to delight in government? If government facilitates you fulfilling your mission in life, in exercising dominion over the earth through employment and provision for your family, and in having a family, are you not going to love and delight in government? It's not the government that grants these rights. Instead, the government is obligated by God to recognize these rights. The government does not impart these things. They are already ours by God, and the government must recognize them.

Now that sets clear limits on governmental authority. When the government gets in the way of man accomplishing his God-given mission, it is no longer functioning as God intended. It is failing to facilitate, and is actually opposing, the kingdom mandate that we have been given by God. That brings us to the purpose of the government, which allows us to ask whether or not government lockdowns are consistent with the God-ordained role for governing authorities.

THE PURPOSE OF GOVERNMENT

Third is *the Purpose of Government.* Verses 3-4: "Rulers are not a cause of fear for good behavior, but for evil. Do you want to have no fear of authority? Do what is good and you will have praise from the same; for it is a minister of God to you for good. But if you do what is evil, be afraid; for it does not bear the sword for nothing; for it is a minister of God, an avenger who brings wrath on the one who practices evil."

As we would expect, the purpose of government is to praise good behavior and avenge evil. That raises an obvious question: Who determines what is good and what is evil? The answer is evident in both Romans 13:1 and the passages we just saw in Genesis: God does. By what? By His Word. If you look at the Ten Commandments, it's easy to see how they relate to the kingdom mandate: "you shall not murder" touches on the right to life; "you shall not commit adultery" touches on the right to family; "you shall not bear false witness against your neighbor" because such falsehood might expose them to unjust liabilities and even death; "you shall not steal" protects a person's property and possessions. That Paul has these things in mind is evident in verses 8-10: "Owe nothing to anyone except to love one another; for he who loves his neighbor has fulfilled the law. For this, 'You shall not commit adultery, you shall not murder, you shall not steal, you shall not covet,' and if there is any other commandment, it is summed up in this saying, 'You shall love your neighbor as yourself.'"

So good and evil are not defined by the ever-evolving whims of culture; good and evil are defined by God. That reinforces the obligation of governments to govern in accord with God's will, an obligation for which they will be judged. This means the limits and purpose of a government are clear. The role of a government is to protect the undeniable rights given to man at creation, and it fulfills this purpose by upholding law and order, punishing evil, and getting out of the way.

We live in a fallen world where the presence of viruses is inevitable. Though the government has the responsibility to protect the right to life of its citizens, its ability to preserve public health is clearly limited—especially against a microscopic pathogen. In this case, we contend that the oppressive restrictions and lockdowns were simply not warranted by the actual threat. More importantly, there are other God-given rights the government is duty-bound to protect: the rights to worship, to work, and to have a family. When civil authorities trample on those fundamental freedoms in the name of public health, they have deviated from their biblical responsibility. The citizens of this nation have been prevented from going to work, from visiting extended family members, and from worshipping corporately in church. These restrictive measures are representative of a kind of oppression that does not honor God.

In fact, if you listen to our government officials, you will notice they talk about trying to balance the infringement on our civil liberties with the harms stemming from the lockdowns. That is an acknowledgment they are stepping outside of their God-ordained lane. In effect, the government is seeking to play the role of God. Only God is sovereign over death and disease. In a push to protect people from an uncontrollable virus, the government has stripped its citizens of their God-given rights and subjected them to all kinds of suffering. What is their justification? That our health system *could* become overwhelmed. What is amazing is that our government actually acknowledges the harms of lockdown measures. Think about that: Governing authorities recognize there are harms resulting from their actions.

Is the virus the government's fault? No, of course not. To our knowledge, our government has no culpability regarding the presence of the virus. So, if someone should die from COVID-19, is the government culpable? The answer is no! We live in a fallen world, and viruses and death are inevitable in a fallen world. A virus has been unleashed on the world, and God is sovereign over that virus. The effects of that virus are not the government's responsibility.

But what if someone dies as a result of governmental lockdown measures? Does that bring culpability before God? I would say yes. Why? Because the government has stepped outside of its God-ordained role. It is no longer functioning in accord with its God-intended purpose. Therefore, the harms that result from such actions fall to them as their responsibility. They will have to give an account to God for those harms. That is significant.

What should government officials have done? In our opinion, they should have equipped Albertans with the best information they have and continued to protect their inalienable rights to work, to worship, to be with family, and to live. The risk from the virus falls to each individual.

What does this mean for our government? Our government needs to repent. If there are believers in our government, they ought to stand up for what's right. Believers everywhere need to start standing for righteousness and calling the people above them to the right standard, even calling them to repentance.

Those in government who do not know Christ need to turn from their sin and believe on Him. They are storing up wrath for themselves for the Day of Judgment. There is a judgment coming and it will be unleashed with the full fury of God's wrath. Those who are in government right now have a responsibility, a heightened accountability. They have a God-ordained function. They are ministers of God and they will be held accountable for the way they carry out that stewardship. If they do not repent, they will be fully held to account before God.

It is not too late to speak up. Put the politics aside. Deal honestly with the situation. I would just appeal to those in government. God is gracious and merciful, slow to anger. If they would confess their sin, acknowledge that they have come short of His glory, and look to His Son, the Lord Jesus Christ, forgiveness is offered to them. The Lord Jesus went to the cross and suffered under the wrath of God for all who would ever believe in His name. God says, "Come, let us reason together" (Isaiah 1:18). If they would come to Christ, they will be forgiven and cleansed and washed. They would be given a new heart, born from above. They would also have everything they need to stand for righteousness, so that they might appeal to those who are with them and above them to do the right thing.

What about law enforcement personnel? They also need to stand for righteousness. If directed to do something wrong, law enforcement workers ought to say to the people above them, "No, I'm not going to do that." They have that responsibility. There are people out there willing to take a stand. We have been contacted by the RCMP in other provinces. There are those in the RCMP who are trying to get their comrades to see things differently. Law enforcement workers need to take a stand and do the right thing.

Let's bring this home. The source of government authority is God. Governing authorities are accountable to Him, and He will hold them accountable in accordance with His Word. There are limits on government authority because the government has a particular purpose, a role and function, that goes all the way back to creation. Governments are in place to uphold and protect the inalienable rights given to us by God; therefore, the government at present needs to cease with its oppressive lockdown measures and instead, protect the rights and freedoms of the people of this province.

More importantly, and what I would want even more than that, is that they would come to a saving knowledge of the Lord Jesus Christ. In fact, I need to proclaim to you the good news. This good news is good only because there is bad news. The bad news is you were born in sin. You came into this world, dead in trespasses and sins. Your heart came into this world hostile to God, hostile to His righteousness, and hostile to His Son. Truth be told, coming into this world, you hated God. If you are outside of Christ, then you hate God now. You may think it is indifference, but in reality, it is hatred and hostility toward God, the One who gives you life and breath right now.

Here is the good news: God sent His Son, to take upon Himself human flesh, to live a life under the law of God, the law of His Father, and He obeyed that law in every respect. He was tempted in all things as we are, yet without sin. In obedience to the Father, He not only lived a perfect life, He went to the cross to offer Himself as a sacrifice for sin. The Father treated the Son, on the cross, as though the Son had committed the sin of all who would ever believe in His name. The perfect, eternal, unblemished, obedient Son was treated on that cross as though He were guilty of the sin of everyone for whom He died. After accomplishing that, He gave up His last breath, on His own authority, went into the grave, and on His own authority, rose from the dead. He is now seated at the right hand of God.

The message of Christ, given to you this day by an ambassador of Christ, is that if you turn from your sin and believe on the Lord Jesus Christ, you will be saved. You will be imputed with the righteousness of Christ, which means you will be clothed with His righteousness. You will be given a perfect record of righteousness so you can stand before God, holy and blameless. You will be given eternal life, and even now you will begin to experience the life of God in your inner man as you are transformed into the image of Christ. That life will carry you into eternity when you die and enter the life to come. You will have hope everlasting and joy unspeakable. You will be in the presence and glory of the Savior for all of eternity, which is not merely a spiritual existence. It is a physical reality, with the new heavens, the new earth, and new glorified bodies fit for eternity. There, you will work, worship, and fellowship as part of His family, exercising all your God-given rights in honor and glory to Him.

CHAPTER 15

CHRIST, COURAGE, AND NONCOMPLIANCE

Nathan Busenitz

This chapter is adapted from a sermon preached at Grace Community Church on the morning of March 14, 2021.

As evangelical Protestants, we belong to a rich heritage of Bible-believing Christians. Both the term *evangelical* and the term *Protestant* come from the sixteenth-century Reformation. And they are both good terms—one positive, and the other negative. One identifies *what we are for*, and the other *what we are against*.

Evangelical was the term Martin Luther used to describe the churches of the Reformation. Of course, he didn't invent the term. Instead, he took the Greek word *euangellion*—which means "gospel," or "good news"—and turned it into an adjective: For the Reformers, the evangelical church represented the church of the true gospel, in contrast to the Roman Catholic errors of the day.

William Tyndale brought the term into English in 1531, and it has been in use ever since. To be evangelical—at least in the historic usage of that term—is to be characterized by the declaration and defense of the gospel of Jesus Christ. For the Reformers, this meant recovering the biblical gospel after centuries of medieval, sacramental tradition had obscured it.

True evangelicalism is still characterized by that same conviction: a commitment to both the purity and the proclamation of the good news of the Lord Jesus—that sinners can be saved by grace through faith in Him alone. For us as evangelicals, the biblical gospel defines who we are and what we are for.

By contrast, the term *Protestant* reflects what we are against. And it too is a historic term, going back to the Reformation. In March 1529, the Second Diet of Speyer convened to determine whether or not the government of the Holy Roman Empire would grant religious tolerance to Luther and the evangelical church. When the Diet of Speyer ruled to ban Luther's teachings and reject his reforms, a group of German princes who were evangelical wrote a letter of protestation to appeal the decision. As their letter of protestation made clear, they rejected the imperial ruling because their consciences were bound to follow the Scriptures. They were willing to disobey a government edict in order to obey God.

This protestation gave rise to the term *Protestant*. Significantly, their protest was not primarily aimed at Roman Catholic error, though that was certainly a factor. Rather, it was a protest against the imperial government, which threatened to interfere in matters of biblical doctrine and Christian worship. To be Protestant, then, was to say to the emperor and to an imperial council that we will not submit to a decree that prevents us from worshipping God in the way He has commanded us to do so in His Word.

That Protestant stand was nothing new. It flowed from an understanding that Christ alone is the head of the church—a conviction articulated by both the Reformers and men like Wycliffe and Huss, who preceded them. Because Christ is supreme over the church, His Word is the authority for the church. The Reformers were convinced that no pope, nor emperor, nor council, nor government agency has the right to interfere in how the church conducts its worship. That is not the jurisdiction of the civil government. It belongs to Christ alone.

This Protestant conviction characterized not only the Reformation, but those who followed in its wake. In England, for example, the Anglican church merely replaced the pope with a king—with Parliament declaring the king of England to be the supreme head of the Church of England. The English Puritans resisted this notion on the grounds that Christ alone is the head of the church. In the early seventeenth century, King James I and his son Charles mandated that the Book of Common Prayer be used in every church in England. The Book of Common Prayer regulated the way in which Anglican worship services were conducted, and it included liturgical elements that were still very Roman Catholic. The Puritans resisted this intrusion from the government of England. In fact, it was this heavy-handed governmental overreach that caused thousands of Puritans to flee from England and come to New England in the 1620s and 1630s. They came in order to worship God in a biblically faithful way, free from governmental opposition.

In the 1640s and 1650s, the Puritans enjoyed a temporary reprieve during the English Civil War and the time of the Protectorate. But when Charles II was restored to the throne in 1660, he again insisted that the Book of Common Prayer govern the worship of every church in England. In 1662, this demand became official when Parliament passed the Act of Uniformity.

Roughly 2,500 Puritan pastors lost their jobs because they refused to comply. They would not allow the king to dictate how the church ought to worship. As a result, they lost their licenses and their pulpits and became known as nonconformists. Those who continued to preach or conduct worship services without permission were prosecuted. One of the most well-known examples was John Bunyan, the famous author of *The Pilgrim's Progress*, who was imprisoned for twelve years because he would not agree to stop preaching.

Several decades earlier, in Scotland, Presbyterians had gathered to sign a national covenant in which they affirmed that Christ alone is the head of the church, and therefore the king had no right to mandate how their churches engaged in worship. They became known as the Scottish Covenanters, and they too rejected the Book of Common Prayer.

As a result, many were severely persecuted by British monarchs. For a season in the 1670s and 1680s, the situation in Scotland was described simply as "The Killing Time," during which Covenant-ers were hunted down by agents of the British Crown. For the Puri-tans and Covenanters, to be Protestant meant to resist and reject any human authority that usurped the place that Christ alone holds as head of the church. No pope, no emperor, no king, no govern-ment official is the head of the church. Only Christ is the head of the church.

This history is, of course, relevant to our situation today. We can hear the echoes of those who came before us when we say, in our own day, that although we respect and submit to the author-ity of government in civil matters, when it comes to the manner in which the church conducts its worship, the government has no jurisdiction here. Christ alone is the head of the church. Therefore, we will obey Him, and worship Him in accordance with His Word above all other authorities. Such an assertion may sound startling to many around us. But it is not contrary to our heritage as Protes-tants—in fact, it lies at the very core of what it has always meant to be Protestant.

Consequently, we might ask: If Scripture commands believers not to forsake the assembly, does the government have the author-ity to tell churches not to assemble, or to assemble only in part? If Scripture commands believers to lift their collective voices in praise to the Lord, does the government have the right to forbid con-gregational singing? If the New Testament describes fellowship in ways that necessitate physical proximity and that include expres-sions of affection and care, is it the government's place to mandate that churches keep people socially isolated from one another? Or to ask the question more broadly, If Scripture declares the Lord Jesus to be the head of the church, is it appropriate for the government to interfere in the way the church of Christ worships her Lord?

Historically speaking, were you to ask such questions of the Reformers, the English Puritans, or the Scottish Covenanters, the answer would have been immediate and resolute: No. Because Christ alone is the head of the church, the governments of this world have no jurisdiction over the worship of His people. And so when we assemble together, even on a day like today, we do so out of the conviction that we must obey God rather than men. The evangelical Protestant movement has always been marked by its gospel courage. As evangelicals, we are for the gospel. It is the substance of our message and the essence of our mission. As Protestants, we courageously stand against the notion that any authority, religious or secular, would usurp the rightful place of the Lord Jesus as the head of the church.

Gospel courage, then, is what ought to define us. Anything less falls short of our Protestant evangelical heritage. More importantly, it falls short of the biblical standard. This kind of courage is not merely something we see in church history. We find equally compelling examples in Scripture, from Daniel to John the Baptist to the apostle Paul. The book of Acts is filled with such examples. One particularly compelling example is found in Acts 5, a text I would like us to consider in more detail.

THE BACKGROUND TO ACTS 5

Before digging into Acts 5 itself, we should first consider the context. The events recorded in this chapter take place sometime within the first two years of the church's inauguration on the Day of Pentecost. In all likelihood, it had only been a few months since the birth of the church.

Acts 2 details that momentous event at Pentecost, when Peter delivered a powerful sermon resulting in the conversion of some 3,000 souls. In Acts 3, Peter and John healed a lame man at the temple. Peter then preached a second resounding sermon, and many more were added to the church. In Acts 4, Peter and John were hauled in front of the religious leaders and strictly warned not to preach in the name of Jesus. The apostles' reply in verses 19-20 is classic: "Whether it is right in the sight of God to give heed to you rather than to God, you be the judge; for we cannot stop speaking about what we have seen and heard."

After being threatened and released, Peter and John returned to the church in Jerusalem, where fellow believers prayed that the Lord would continue to give them boldness. The words of that specific intercession are instructive: "And now, Lord, take note of their threats, and grant that Your bond-servants may speak Your word with all confidence" (verse 29). I love that. In the face of hostility and opposition, give us boldness to speak Your word with confidence. What a prayer request!

When we come to Acts 5, we will see that prayer request answered. Chapter 5, then, opens with the story of Ananias and Sapphira, a sobering reminder that God is not mocked and that He desires His church to be pure. In verses 12-16, we see that the Lord was clearly blessing the work of the apostles and the ministry of the Jerusalem church. In keeping with their foundational role as apostles, Peter and his associates performed healing miracles—signs that authenticated their apostolic ministry and validated their gospel message. According to verse 14, the church was growing rapidly, with multitudes of new believers constantly joining. In fact, the apostles were so popular that people were traveling from all around Jerusalem to be healed by them and to hear them preach. As noted above, in Acts 4:29, they had prayed for gospel courage. Now, starting in Acts 5:17, the courage they prayed for would be put to the test.

That, then, brings us to our text in Acts 5:17-42. As we unpack these verses, I'd like to organize our thoughts around two big questions: First, what does gospel courage look like? Second, what are the ingredients that make such courage possible? In other words, what elements are needed to cultivate that kind of courage in our lives today?

WHAT DOES GOSPEL COURAGE LOOK LIKE?

Acts 5 answers that question by recording the compelling example of the apostles. As we think about their example, we will focus on three characteristics of their courage: In verses 17-26, they exhibit the courage to speak. In verses 18-39, they demonstrate the courage to stand. And finally, in verses 40-42, they exemplify the courage to suffer. We will consider each of these in more detail as we go through the text.

The Courage to Speak (verses 17-26)

In verses 17-21, Luke writes:

> The high priest rose up, along with all his associates (that is the sect of the Sadducees), and they were filled with jealousy. They laid hands on the apostles and put them in a public jail. But during the night an angel of the Lord opened the gates of the prison, and taking them out he said, "Go, stand and speak to the people in the temple the whole message of this Life." Upon hearing this, they entered into the temple about daybreak and began to teach.

The apostles, of course, had done nothing wrong. Yet the religious rulers had them arrested and imprisoned—they were jealous that the people were being drawn to them. In Acts 4:17-18, Peter and John had been warned to stop preaching. Now they, along with the rest of the apostles, have been arrested and imprisoned. But their incarceration does not last long.

As He will do again in Acts 12, God sent an angel during the night to open the prison doors so the apostles could leave. But this is not your typical escape. The angel does not instruct them to go into witness protection or flee from Jerusalem. The counterintuitive instruction is simple: Go back to the temple and keep preaching the very message that got you locked up in the first place. "Go, stand and speak to the people in the temple the whole message of this Life" (verse 20). I love that description of the gospel: "the whole message of this Life."

What do the apostles do? They immediately returned to the temple so that even as the sun was just beginning to come up, they were back in the same spot proclaiming the truth about Jesus Christ. Admittedly, the circumstances here are extraordinary, with supernatural prison breaks and angelic imperatives. Nonetheless, we should not overlook the apostles' bold obedience as they open their mouths and speak out for the sake of Christ. They had been warned by the religious leaders not to preach Jesus. They had been imprisoned for preaching about Jesus. They knew they would likely be arrested again if they proclaimed the name of Jesus. So what do they do? They preach Jesus!

Their example of courage is compelling because they were willing to *speak up* and *speak out* even though they knew they could face serious repercussions from governing officials for doing so. It is this kind of courage that Christ calls us to as His followers—the courage that speaks the truth even when the world does not want to listen. The apostles went to the temple and they began to preach.

Meanwhile, back at the jail, chaos erupted when the soldiers went to collect their prisoners and nobody was home. Luke tells us what happened next:

> Now when the high priest and his associates came, they called the Council together, even all the Senate of the sons of Israel, and sent orders to the prison house for

them to be brought. But the officers who came did not find them in the prison; and they returned and reported back, saying, "We found the prison house locked quite securely and the guards standing at the doors; but when we had opened up, we found no one inside." Now when the captain of the temple guard and the chief priests heard these words, they were greatly perplexed about them as to what would come of this. But someone came and reported to them, "The men whom you put in prison are standing in the temple and teaching the people!" Then the captain went along with the officers and proceeded to bring them back without violence (for they were afraid of the people, that they might be stoned) (Acts 5:21-26).

Verse 24 highlights the perplexity of both the religious leaders and the officers. How amazed they must have been to learn that not only was the prison empty, but their prisoners were back in the temple, not in hiding but preaching publicly. The audacity of these followers of Jesus!

Notice how the courage of the apostles is contrasted (in verse 26) with the fear of the soldiers. Normally, it's the fugitives who are afraid. But not on this occasion. The soldiers are afraid, while the apostles are courageous. When told to stop preaching, the apostles refused to comply. They responded instead with gospel courage and boldly proclaimed the good news of Jesus Christ.

The Courage to Stand (verses 27-39)

The narrative continues in verses 27-28. There, we read, "When they had brought them, they stood them before the Council. The high priest questioned them, saying, 'We gave you strict orders not to continue teaching in this name, and yet, you have filled Jerusalem with your teaching and intend to bring this man's blood upon us.'"

Only a few months earlier, Peter and his fellow apostles had fled when Jesus was arrested in the garden. Peter had followed the soldiers from a distance, making his way to the courtyard of the high priest's house. There, he denied his Lord three times, acting rashly out of fear and cowardice. Here, just months later, he stands before that same high priest—the same religious leaders who sentenced his Master to be crucified—and he hears them say, in essence, "We told you to stop preaching, and you did not comply. As a result, you have filled Jerusalem with the message of Jesus, whom we sentenced to death. What do you have to say for yourselves?"

How will Peter respond? Will he flee? Will he deny his Lord? Not this time. As Luke records,

> Peter and the apostles answered, "We must obey God rather than men. The God of our fathers raised up Jesus, whom you had put to death by hanging Him on a cross. He is the one whom God exalted to His right hand as a Prince and a Savior, to grant repentance to Israel, and forgiveness of sins. And we are witnesses of these things; and so is the Holy Spirit, whom God has given to those who obey Him" (verses 29-32).

We will consider Peter's answer in a bit more detail later, but what I want to point out here is the resolve we hear in Peter's words. He does not back down or shrink away or make excuses or apologize. Not for a second. Rather, he looks at the council of religious leaders and says, in essence, "We are men under authority from God. And His authority trumps your authority. Therefore, with all due respect, we cannot comply with your prohibition. For our duty to obey God and carry out His will transcends our obligation to listen to you." What courage! Peter boldly defies the council by appealing to an authority greater than theirs.

Again, the apostles' example is compelling for us. On what basis can we have the courage to stand up in the public square and say that truth is absolute, and Christ alone saves, and hell is real, and naturalistic evolution is false, and homosexuality is sinful, and gender is determined at birth? We can do so because we have the Word of God, which comes with His very authority. And therefore, we appeal to an authority that is higher than any other authority. And on that basis, we say with Peter, "We must obey God rather than men."

For Peter and the other apostles, this bold stand almost cost them their lives. The passage continues:

> When they [the religious leaders] heard this, they were cut to the quick and intended to kill them. But a Pharisee named Gamaliel, a teacher of the Law, respected by all the people, stood up in the Council and gave orders to put the men outside for a short time. And he said to them, "Men of Israel, take care what you propose to do with these men. For some time ago Theudas rose up, claiming to be somebody, and a group of about four hundred men joined up with him. But he was killed, and all who followed him were dispersed and came to nothing. After this man, Judas of Galilee rose up in the days of the census and drew away some people after him; he too perished, and all those who followed him were scattered. So in the present case, I say to you, stay away from these men and let them alone, for if this plan or action is of men, it will be overthrown; but if it is of God, you will not be able to overthrow them; or else you may even be found fighting against God" (verses 33-39).

Verses 33-39 provide an interesting interlude in the narrative. Gamaliel's words are almost parenthetical, so why did Luke include them in his narrative? I believe there are a few reasons: First, Gamaliel's words explain why the apostles were not executed that day when it looked like they probably would be. Second and more importantly, Gamaliel's speech highlights a basic theological truth: namely, that if God is at work in something, human beings will not be able to thwart Him. The short-lived movements of Theudas and Judas of Galilee, self-professed deliverers of Israel, were clearly not of God because they disintegrated into nothing. Those movements stand in contrast to the permanence of the Jesus movement. Finally, Gamaliel's warning to his fellow leaders is that if this movement is from God, and we fight against it, we will be fighting against God. This provides a somewhat ironic backdrop for later persecutions against the church, in which the religious leaders did in fact resist God's work.

The clearest example of this is Saul, prior to his conversion on the Damascus Road. Significantly, according to Acts 22:3, Saul was a student of Gamaliel. In Saul's crusade against Christians, he ignored his own mentor's advice. In Acts 9, on his way to Damascus, he was suddenly confronted with the truth that he had been fighting against God. In this way, Gamaliel's testimony serves as a condemnation of the unbelief of the religious leaders, who repeatedly resisted the work of God.

Coming back to the primary point we are making in this section: Peter and his fellow apostles demonstrated the courage to stand firm in the face of persecution. When confronted with the hostility of an incredulous governing authority, the apostles demonstrated gospel courage. Their boldness to stand firm and not back down did not stem from their own inner fortitude or personal resolve. It was fueled by their unwavering commitment to obey God first and foremost. Their obedience to Him demanded their disobedience to the religious leaders. Because they feared God, they did not fear man.

The Courage to Suffer (verses 40-42)

The final three verses of Acts 5 bring this dramatic scene to a close. Luke writes:

They took his advice; and after calling the apostles in, they flogged them and ordered them not to speak in the name of Jesus, and then released them. So they went on their way from the presence of the Council, rejoicing that they had been considered worthy to suffer shame for His name. And every day, in the temple and from house to house, they kept right on teaching and preaching Jesus as the Christ (verses 40-42).

Based on Gamaliel's advice, the religious leaders relented from their initial desire to kill the apostles. Instead, they had them flogged, meaning they were given 39 lashes with a whip, in keeping with the protocols outlined in Deuteronomy 25:1-3. Severe but not lethal, flogging was intended to send a strong message: stop preaching or you will receive worse.

How did the apostles respond? First, they rejoiced in their suffering—not because getting severely whipped is enjoyable, but because they were counted worthy to suffer for the sake of Christ. To suffer for His sake is an act of worship, service, and fidelity to Him. In that, there is great reward. And so they rejoiced.

Not only that, but, as verse 42 explains, "every day, in the temple and from house to house, they kept right on teaching and preaching Jesus as the Christ." They refused to be intimidated by the threats of the religious leaders. They did not stop for even a day. They kept preaching in the temple. They kept teaching from house to house. They kept proclaiming Jesus as the Messiah. They kept right on doing it because they understood that it is better to obey God than men.

So we see that they suffered well on two counts. First, they found joy in the opportunity to suffer for the sake of their Savior—the One who had suffered so much more for them. Second, they suffered well because they did not allow the suffering to deter them from obedience to Christ. Rather than being intimidated, their suffering only increased their resolve. What a compelling example of gospel courage. Gladly, they suffered. Boldly, they obeyed.

WHAT ARE THE INGREDIENTS
FOR THIS KIND OF COURAGE?

Acts 5 gives us a compelling illustration of what it looks like to exhibit gospel courage—the courage to speak out for Christ, to stand firm for Him, and to suffer well for His sake. But how can we cultivate this same kind of courage in our hearts? What are the ingredients that make this kind of courage possible?

The answer to that question is found back in verses 29-32, in Peter's reply to the council. There, Peter declared,

> We must obey God rather than men. The God of our fathers raised up Jesus, whom you had put to death by hanging Him on a cross. He is the one whom God exalted to His right hand as a Prince and a Savior, to grant repentance to Israel, and forgiveness of sins. And we are witnesses of these things; and so is the Holy Spirit, whom God has given to those who obey Him (Acts 5:29-32).

Peter's answer highlights the three core ingredients of gospel courage. How were Peter and the other apostles able to respond with such courage in the face of fierce opposition?

First, they recognized their God-given mandate: "We must obey God rather than men" (verse 29). This was not an option; it was an obligation. And it came from the highest possible authority, God Himself. As the apostles understood, obedience to God is far more important than the fear of man. Simply by being obedient, they proved themselves to be courageous.

Second, they reiterated their Christ-centered message. Peter's answer includes the essential components of the gospel message. He notes the death, resurrection, ascension, exaltation, and exclusivity of Christ. His words also highlight the need for repentance and the reality of forgiveness. Peter and his fellow apostles were on message. They had personally been transformed by that message. As Paul said in 2 Corinthians 4:13, "We also believe, therefore we also speak." These apostles believed, and therefore they could not stay silent.

Third, they rested in their Spirit-empowered mission. According to Acts 1:8, the apostles' mission was to be witnesses to the truth about the Lord Jesus. Here in Acts 5:32, they rest in the fact that their witness is empowered by the Holy Spirit, who is given by God to those who obey Him. The word for "witness" there in verse 32 is *martoos*, a Greek word from which we get the English word *martyr*. A martyr is a witness of Jesus Christ, even to the point of death. Peter and his fellow apostles boldly declare to the religious leaders, "We are witnesses of Jesus Christ. And as we seek to accomplish our mission, we do so with the confidence that we are empowered by the Holy Spirit."

For Peter and his fellow apostles, their courage was grounded in their God-given mandate, their Christ-centered message, and their Spirit-empowered mission. Now, someone might say, "Well, that was good for the apostles." But as believers, we possess those same three ingredients for gospel courage. First, we have also been given a mandate, a commission, to go into the world and make disciples by teaching them all that Christ has commanded us. Those commandments are found in God's Word, which is the supreme authority for what we believe and how we live. Second, we know the gospel message, because it is the very truth that we have embraced in saving faith. We, too, are called to be witnesses to Christ and explain the wonder of His mercy and grace to those who are perishing. Third, like the apostles, we have the Holy Spirit, who indwells us, and who empowers His Word so that when we proclaim the gospel it does not return void. Our courage is grounded in the knowledge that He who is in us is greater than he who is in the world.

By remembering our God-given mandate, our Christ-centered message, and our Spirit-empowered mission, we can exhibit the same kind of gospel courage that the apostles demonstrated so powerfully here in Acts 5—the courage to speak, to stand, and to suffer for Christ. We tend to think that we have to muster up some kind of internal fortitude in order to be courageous. In reality, all we have to do is be obedient and live out our biblical convictions with consistency—even when it becomes unpopular to do so.

When Peter stood before the hostile religious leaders, he wasn't focused on being bold. He was focused on being obedient to the Lord. The result was courage, but it was courage that flowed from his God-honoring convictions. The same is true for us. Gospel courage is grounded in the gospel. It flows from hearts that have been transformed by God's grace, and it is seen in lives that are committed to obeying Him no matter the cost.

ACKNOWLEDGMENTS

This project would not have been possible without the help of family, friends, and fellow workers. Nathan would like to thank his wife, Beth, and his family for their constant support. He is also deeply grateful for the courage and constancy demonstrated by the elders of Grace Community Church. It is a joy to serve alongside you. Special thanks to John MacArthur, Chris Hamilton, Phil Johnson, Mark Zhakevich, Austin Duncan, Mike Riccardi, Hohn Cho, Carl Hargrove, and George Crawford for their feedback and encouragement.

James would like to thank his wife, Erin. The stand that was taken would have been near impossible without her unwavering support. Also critical to this stand were his fellow church leaders: Mike Hovland, Jacob Spenst, Paul Claassen, Brad Bredenhof, Adam Pillidge, Mark Blackburn, and Rob Chomiak. Your steadfast commitment to the lordship and headship of Christ is undeniable. To the congregation at GraceLife, you are a precious expression of the bride of Christ. To Isaac and Caleb, you are dearly beloved sons who sacrificed much.

Additionally, we would like to express our gratitude to our respective legal teams for their advice pertaining to this volume. A special word of thanks also goes to Bob Hawkins and Steve Miller of Harvest House Publishers. Steve invested countless hours in the editing process, and we are grateful for his help. Finally, we wish to express our gratitude to the Lord, committing this project to Him. To Him be the glory.

NOTES

1. For example, see Adam T. Biggs and Lanny F. Littlejohn, "Revisiting the initial COVID-19 pandemic projections," *The Lancet Microbe* 2/3, March 1, 2021, https://www.thelancet.com/journals/lanmic/article/PIIS2666-5247(21)00029-X/fulltext. This article is linked by the National Library of Medicine at https://pubmed.ncbi.nlm.nih.gov/33942033/. See also John P.A. Loannidis, "Coronavirus disease 2019: The harms of exaggerated information and non-evidence-based measures," April 9, 2020, posted by the National Institute of Health at https://www.ncbi.nlm.nih.gov/pmc/articles/PMC7163529/. For a study demonstrating that roughly half of those hospitalized do not exhibit severe symptoms, see David Zweig, "Our Most Reliable Pandemic Number Is Losing Meaning: A new study suggests that almost half of those hospitalized with COVID-19 have mild or asymptomatic cases," *The Atlantic*, Sept. 13, 2021, https://www.theatlantic.com/health/archive/2021/09/covid-hospitalization-numbers-can-be-misleading/620062/.

2. See John MacArthur, "Act Like Men," preached June 21, 2020. Transcript available from Grace to You, online at https://www.gty.org/library/sermons-library/81-82/act-like-men.

3. John MacArthur, "How Should Christians Respond to the Riots?," preached June 14, 2020. Transcript available from Grace to You, online at https://www.gty.org/library/sermons-library/81-81/how-should-christians-respond-to-the-riots.

4. For example, in an August 2020 journal article posted on the US National Library of Medicine/National Institute of Health website, researchers from Stanford, Northwestern, and the University of Sidney wrote the following: "Early on, experienced modelers drew parallels between COVID-19 and the Spanish flu that caused >50 million deaths with mean age of death being 28. We all lament the current loss of life. However, as of June 18, the total fatalities are ~450,000 with median age ~80 and typically multiple comorbidities. Brilliant scientists expected 100,000,000 cases accruing within 4 weeks in the USA. Predictions for hospital and ICU bed requirements were also entirely misinforming. Public leaders trusted models (sometimes even black boxes without disclosed methodology) inferring massively overwhelmed health care capacity. However, very few hospitals were eventually stressed and only for a couple of weeks. Most hospitals maintained largely empty wards, expecting tsunamis that never came." John P.A. Loanmidis, Sally Cripps, and Martin A. Tanner, "Forecasting for COVID-19 has failed," August 25, 2020. Article posted online at: https://www.ncbi.nlm.nih.gov/pmc/articles/PMC7447267/.

5. Addendum to "Christ, Not Caesar, Is the Head of the Church," July 24, 2020, published on the Grace Community Church website, online at: https://www.gracechurch.org/news/posts/1988.

6. "Christ, Not Caesar, Is the Head of the Church," July 24, 2020, published on the Grace Community Church website, online at https://www.gracechurch.org/news/posts/1988.

7. John MacArthur, "We Must Obey God Rather Than Men," sermon preached July 26, 2020. Transcript available from Grace to You, online at https://www.gty.org/library/sermons-library/81-87/we-must-obey-god-rather-than-men.

8. "Los Angeles church, pastor win in court Friday, can continue indoor services judge rules," *Contra Costa Herald*, August 14, 2020, https://contracostaherald.com/los-angeles-church-pastor-win-in-court-friday-can-continue-indoor-services-judge-rules/.

9. Letter sent to Grace Community Church on behalf of the Los Angeles County Department of Public Health, July 29, 2020, https://eadn-wc01-1479010.nxedge.io/cdn/wp-content/uploads/2020/08/MacArthur-Ex.-5-1_Cease-and-Desist-Letter.pdf.

10. As someone who loves church history, I couldn't help but note some irony, since Sir Thomas More persecuted Protestants during the English Reformation. Five centuries later, a law firm bearing his name was fighting to protect the right for Protestants like us to gather for worship each week.

11. Jenna Ellis, cited from "Los Angeles church, pastor win in court Friday, can continue indoor services judge rules." Regarding the pandemic and its effect on mental health and suicidal thoughts, the US Department of Health and Human Services posted an insightful article, dated August 14, 2020. It noted, "Elevated levels of adverse mental health conditions, substance use, and suicidal ideation were reported by adults in the United States in June 2020...Suicidal ideation was also elevated; approximately twice as many respondents reported serious consideration of suicide in the previous 30 days than did adults in the United States in 2018, referring to the previous 12 months (10.7% versus 4.3%)." Czeisler MÉ , Lane RI, Petrosky E, et al, Mental Health, Substance Use, and Suicidal Ideation During the COVID-19 Pandemic — United States, June 24-30, 2020. *Morbidity and Mortality Report Weekly*, https://www.cdc.gov/mmwr/volumes/69/wr/mm6932a1.htm?s_cid=mm6932a1_w#suggestedcitation.

12. The countersuit filed by Los Angeles County can be found online at the following address: http://file.lacounty.gov/SDSInter/lac/1076769_COMPLAINT-ComplaintforViolationofEmergencyHealthOrdersandAbatementofPublicNuisance.pdf?utm_content=&utm_medium=email&utm_name=&utm_source=govdelivery&utm_term=.

13. "Los Angeles church, pastor win in court Friday, can continue indoor services judge rules."

14. The ruling of the California Court of Appeal, dated August 15, 2020, can be found at the following link: https://file.lacounty.gov/SDSInter/lac/1076857_GraceChurchOrder.pdf. For more information, see Jesse T. Jackson, "Grace Community Church Given Permission to Have Services, Then Lost Permission, Again," *Church Leaders*, August 17, 2020, https://churchleaders.com/news/380730-grace-community-church-permission-services.html.

15. John MacArthur in a CNN interview, cited from "Los Angeles County sues San Fernando Valley-based Grace Community Church over indoor services drawing thousands of people," *KTLA 5*, August 13, 2020, https://ktla.com/news/los-angeles-county-sues-san-fernando-valley-based-grace-community-church-over-services-with-thousands/.

16. Cf. Valerie Richardson, "Judge rejects Los Angeles County's effort to hold Grace Community Church in contempt," *The Washington Times* August 20, 2020, https://www.washingtontimes.com/news/2020/aug/20/judge-rejects-los-angeles-countys-effort-hold-grac/.

17. Cf. "Judge mulls LA County's request for temporary restraining order against indoor church services," *Los Angeles Daily News*, August 24, 2020, https://www.dailynews.com/2020/08/24/judge-mulls-la-countys-request-for-temporary-restraining-order-against-indoor-church-services/.

18. Leah MarieAnn Klett, "Judge denies attempts to shutter Grace Community Church; Mac Arthur condemns 'misuse of power,'" *The Christian Post*, August 26, 2020, https://www.christianpost.com/news/judge-denies-attempts-to-shutter-grace-community-church-macarthur-condemns-misuse-of-power.html?uid=10fc0f8f52.

19. "Declaration of Pastor John MacArthur," Los Angeles County Superior Court, August 23, 2020, https://www.thomasmoresociety.org/wp-content/uploads/2020/08/Oppo-to-Ex-Parte-Renewed-TRO_MacArthur-Decl_JMT.pdf.

20. "LA county takes back John MacArthur's parking lot amid dispute over church closure," *Christianity Today*, August 31, 2020, https://www.christiantoday.com/article/la.county.takes.back.john.macarthurs.parking.lot.in.dispute.over.church.closure/135463.htm.

21. See, for example, Debra Bharath, "Judge grants injunction prohibiting Sun Valley church from holding indoor services," *Los Angeles Daily News*, September 10, 2020, https://www.dailynews.com/2020/09/10/judge-grants-injunction-prohibiting-sun-valley-church-from-holding-indoor-services/.

22. "MacArthur Prevails—California Court Says Church and Pastor Entitled to Trial," *The Thomas More Society*, September 24, 2020, https://thomasmoresociety.org/macarthur-prevails-california-court-says-church-and-pastor-entitled-to trial/.

23. "MacArthur Prevails—California Court Says Church and Pastor Entitled to Trial."

24. "Big Religious Liberty Win for John MacArthur and Grace Church," *The Thomas More Society*, September 1, 2021, https://thomasmoresociety.org/big-religious-liberty-win-for-john-macarthur-and-grace-church/.

25. Nathan Busenitz, "We Stand with Pastor James Coates," *The Master's Seminary*, February 23, 2021, https://blog.tms.edu/we-stand-with-pastor-james-coates.

26. Madeline Osburn, "The Scientist Whose Doomsday Pandemic Model Predicted Armageddon Just Walked Back the Apocalyptic Predictions," *The Federalist*, March 26, 2020, https://thefederalist.com/2020/03/26/the-scientist-whose-doomsday-pandemic-model-predicted-armageddon-just-walked-back-the-apocalyptic-predictions/.

27. Waterbreak with The Waterboy is a podcast done by Gabriel Rench. His show has given a lot of visibility to the battle in Canada. He has had a number of Canadian pastors on his show. The interview in question can be seen here: https://www.youtube.com/watch?v=UqVnUHE3fuo.

28. See at https://www.youtube.com/watch?v=0ywfs4rQipQ.

29. See at https://www.youtube.com/watch?v=71we5acBrHc.

30. The video states that pastor Jacob Spenst preached that Sunday, but it was in fact Mike Hovland. See at https://www.rebelnews.com/pastor_james_returns_to_gracelife_rcmp_try_to_disrupt_services.

31. "Justice Centre obtains change to expansive Court ban on all peaceful outdoor gatherings in Alberta," *Justice Centre*, May 14, 2021, https://www.jccf.ca/justice-centre-obtains-change-to-expansive-court-ban-on-all-peaceful-outdoor-gatherings-in-alberta/.

32. Though this article announces pastor Tim Stephens's second arrest, it also highlights the underhanded way AHS was functioning even after the original court order had been modified. "Pastor Tim Stephens arrested illegally again," *Justice Centre*, June 15, 2021, https://www.jccf.ca/pastor-tim-stephens-arrested-illegally-again/.

33. See at https://www.youtube.com/watch?v=KkLS6w2bmX8.

34. Martin Luther at the Diet of Worms. Cited from Owen Anderson, "The First Amendment and Natural Religion," 15-44 in *The Cambridge Companion to the First Amendment and Religious Liberty*, eds. Michael D. Briedenbach and Owen Anderson (New York: Cambridge University Press, 2020), 28.

35. "Cases in Alberta," *Alberta*, https://www.alberta.ca/stats/covid-19-alberta-statistics.htm#highlights.

To learn more about Harvest House books and
to read sample chapters, visit our website:

www.HarvestHousePublishers.com

HARVEST HOUSE PUBLISHERS
EUGENE, OREGON